Waterloo

Hilaire Belloc

Waterloo

Copyright © 2020 Bibliotech Press
All rights reserved

The present edition is a reproduction of previous publication of this classic work. Minor typographical errors may have been corrected without note; however, for an authentic reading experience the spelling, punctuation, and capitalization have been retained from the original text.

ISBN: 978-1-63637-028-6

CONTENTS

I	THE POLITICAL OBJECT AND EFFECT OF THE WATERLOO CAMPAIGN	2
II	THE PRELIMINARIES: NAPOLEON'S ADVANCE ACROSS THE SAMBRE	10
III	THE DECISIVE DAY: FRIDAY, THE 16TH OF JUNE—	28
IV	THE ALLIED RETREAT AND FRENCH ADVANCE UPON WATERLOO AND WAVRE	73
V	THE ACTION	91

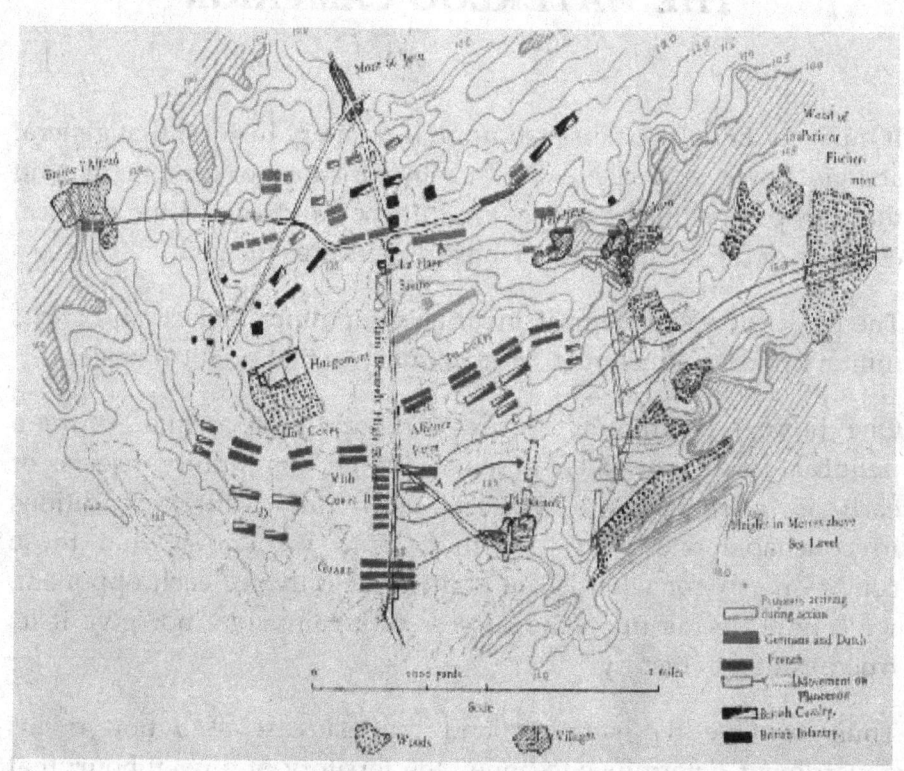

"Coloured" map

I

THE POLITICAL OBJECT AND EFFECT OF THE WATERLOO CAMPAIGN

It must continually be insisted upon in military history, that general actions, however decisive, are but the functions of campaigns; and that campaigns, in their turn, are but the functions of the political energies of the governments whose armies are engaged.

The object of a campaign is invariably a political object, and all its military effort is, or should be, subsidiary to that political object.

One human community desires to impose upon the future a political condition which another human community rejects; or each is attempting to impose upon the future, conditions irreconcilable one with the other. Until we know what those conditions are, or what is the political objective of each opponent, we cannot decide upon the success of a campaign, nor give it its true position in history.

Thus, to take the simplest and crudest case, a nation or its government determines to annex the territory of a neighbour; that is, to subject a neighbouring community to the laws of the conqueror. That neighbouring community and its government, if they are so old-fashioned as to prefer freedom, will resist by force of arms, and there will follow what is called a "campaign" (a term derived from the French, and signifying a countryside: for countrysides are the theatres of wars). In this campaign the political object of the attempted conquest on the one hand, and of resistance to it on the other, are the issue. The military aspect of the campaign is subsidiary to its political objects, and we judge of its success or failure not in military but in political terms.

The prime military object of a general is to "annihilate" the armed force of his opponents. He may do this by breaking up their organisation and dispersing them, or by compelling the surrender of their arms. He may achieve success in this purely military object in any degree. But if, as an end and consequence of his military success, the political object be not achieved—if, for instance, in the particular case we are considering, the neighbouring community does not in the future obey laws dictated to it by the conqueror, but remains autonomous—then the campaign has failed.

Such considerations are, I repeat, the very foundation of military history; and throughout this Series they will be insisted upon as the light in which alone military history can be understood.

It is further true that not only may a campaign be successful in the military sense, and yet in the largest historical sense be a failure, but, quite evidently, the actions in a campaign may each be successful and yet the campaign a failure; or each action may, on the whole, fail, and yet that campaign be a success. As the old formula go, "You can win every battle and lose your campaign." And, again, "A great general does not aim at winning battles, but at winning his campaign." An action results from the contact of the opposing forces, and from the necessity in which they find themselves, after such contact, of attempting the one to disorganise or to capture the other. And in the greater part actions are only "accepted," as the phrase goes, by either party, because each party regards the action as presenting opportunities for his own success.

A campaign can perfectly well be conceived in which an opponent, consciously inferior in the field, will avoid action throughout, and by such a plan can actually win the campaign in the end. Historical instances of this, though rare, exist. And there have even been campaigns where, after a great action disastrous to one side, that side has yet been able to keep up a broken resistance sufficiently lengthy and exhausting to baulk the conqueror of his political object in the end.

In a word, it is the business of the serious student in military history to reverse the popular and dramatic conception of war, to neglect the brilliance and local interest of a battle for the larger view of the whole operations; and, again, to remember that these operations are not an end in themselves, but are only designed to serve the political plan of the government which has commanded them.

Judged in this true light, we may establish the following conclusions with regard to the battle of Waterloo.

First, the battle of Waterloo was a decisive action, the result of which was a complete military success for the Allies in the campaign they had undertaken, and a complete military defeat for Napoleon, who had opposed them.

This complete military success of the Allies' campaign was, again, equivalent to a success in their immediate political object, which was the overthrow of Napoleon's personal power, the re-establishment of the Bourbons upon the French throne, and the restoration of those traditions and ideals of government which had been common to Europe before the outbreak of the French Revolution twenty-four years before.

Had the effect of this battle and that campaign been permanent, one could speak of their success as complete; but when we discuss that largest issue of all, to wit, whether the short campaign which Waterloo so decisively concluded really effected its object, considering that that object was the permanent destruction of the revolutionary effort and the permanent re-establishment of the old state of affairs in Europe, we are compelled to arrive at a very different conclusion: a conclusion which will vary with the varying judgment of men, and one which cannot be final, because the drama is not yet played out; but a conclusion which, in the eyes of all, singularly modifies the effect of the campaign of Waterloo.

It is obvious, at the first glance we take of European history during, say, the lifetime of a man who should have been a boy in Waterloo year, that the general political object of the revolutionary and Napoleonic armies was not reversed at Waterloo. It was ultimately established. The war had been successfully maintained during too long a period for the uprooting of the political conditions which the French had attempted to impose upon Europe. Again, those conditions were sufficiently sympathetic to the European mind at the time to develop generously, and to grow in spite of all attempted restriction. And we discover, as a fact, democratic institutions, democratic machinery at least, spreading rapidly again after their defeat at Waterloo, and partially victorious, first in France and later elsewhere, within a very few years of that action.

The same is true of certain secondary results of the prolonged revolutionary and Napoleonic campaigns. Nationality predominated over the old idea of a monarch governing his various "peoples," and the whole history of the nineteenth century was a gradual vindication of the principle of nationality. A similar fate awaited institutions bound up with the French revolutionary effort: a wide and continually expressed suffrage, the arming of whole nations in defence of their independence, the ordering of political life upon the new plan, down even to the details of the revolutionary weights and measures (the metre, the gramme, etc.)—these succeeded and in effect triumphed over the arrangements which that older society had fought to restore.

On the other hand, the advance of all this was much slower, much more disturbed, much less complete, than it would have been had Napoleon not failed in Russia, suffered his decisive defeat at Leipzig, and fallen for ever upon that famous field of Waterloo; and one particular characteristic, namely, the imposition of all these things upon Europe by the will of a government at Paris, wholly disappeared.

We may sum up, then, and say that the political effect of the battle of Waterloo and its campaign was an immediate success for the Allies: that their ultimate success the history of the nineteenth century has reversed; but that the victory of Waterloo modified, retarded, and perhaps distorted in a permanent fashion the establishment of those conceptions of society and government which the Revolution, and Napoleon as its soldier, had set out to establish.

There is a side question attached to all this, with which I shall conclude, because it forms the best introduction to what is to follow: that question is,—"Would Napoleon have ultimately succeeded even if he had triumphed instead of fallen upon the 18th of June 1815?" In other words, was Waterloo one of these battles the winning or losing of which by *either* side, meant a corresponding decisive result to that side? Had Wellington's command broken at Waterloo before the arrival of Blucher, would Napoleon's consequent victory have meant as much to *him* as his defeat actually meant to the allies?

The answer of history to this question is, No. Even had Napoleon won on that day he would have lost in the long run.

The date to which we must affix the reverse of Napoleon's effort is not the 18th of June 1815, but the 19th of October 1812, when the Grand Army began its retreat from Moscow; and the political decision, his failure in which was the origin of his fall, was not the decision taken in June 1815 to advance against the Allies in Belgium, but the decision taken in May 1812 to advance into the vast spaces of Russia. The decisive action which the largest view of history will record in centuries to come as the defeat which ruined Napoleon took place, not south of Brussels, but near the town of Leipzig, two years before. From the last moment of that three days' battle (again the 19th of October, precisely a twelvemonth after the retreat from Moscow had begun), Napoleon and the French armies are continually falling back. Upon the 4th of April in the following year Napoleon abdicated; and exactly a month later, on the 4th of May, he was imprisoned, under the show of local sovereignty, in the island of Elba.

It was upon the 1st of March 1815 that, having escaped from that island, he landed upon the southern coast of France. There followed the doomed attempt to save somewhat of the Revolution and the Napoleonic scheme, which is known to history as the "hundred days." Even that attempt would have been impossible had not the greater part of the commanders of units in the French army, that is, of the colonels of regiments, abandoned the Bourbon government, which had been restored at Paris, and decided to support Napoleon.

But even so, the experiment was hazardous in the extreme. Had the surrounding governments which had witnessed and triumphed over his fall permitted him, as he desired, to govern France in peace, and France alone, this small part of the revolutionary plan might have been saved from the general wreck of its fortunes and of his. But such an hypothesis is fantastic. There could be and there was no chance that these great governments, now fully armed, and with all their organised hosts prepared and filled with the memory of recent victory, would permit the restoration of democratic government in that France which had been the centre and outset of the vast movement they had determined to destroy. Further, though Napoleon had behind him the majority, he had not the united mass of the French people. An ordered peace following upon victory would have given him such a support; after his recent crushing defeat it was lacking. It was especially true that the great chiefs of the army were doubtful. His own generals rejoined him, some with enthusiasm, more with doubt, while a few betrayed him early in the process of his attempted restoration.

It is impossible to believe that under such circumstances Napoleon could have successfully met Europe in arms. The military resources of the French people, though not exhausted, were reaching their term. New levies of men yielded a material far inferior to the conscripts of earlier years; and when the Emperor estimated 800,000 men as the force which he required for his effort, it was but the calculation of despair. Eight hundred thousand men: even had they been the harvest of a long peace, the whole armed nation, vigorous in health and fresh for a prolonged contest, would not have been sufficient. The combined Powers had actually under arms a number as great as that, and inexhaustible reserves upon which to draw. A quarter of a million stood ready in the Netherlands, another quarter of a million could march from Austria to cross the Rhine. North Italy had actually present against him 70,000 men; and Russia, which had a similarly active and ready force of 170,000, could increase that host almost indefinitely from her enormous body of population.

But, so far from 800,000 men, Napoleon found to his command not one quarter of that number armed and ready for war. Though Napoleon fell back upon that desperate resource of a starved army, the inclusion of militia; though he swept into his net the whole youth of that year, and accepted conscripts almost without regard to physical capacity; though he went so far as to put the sailors upon shore to help him in his effort, and counted in his effectives the police, the customs officials, and, as one may say, every uniformed man, he was compelled, even after two and a half months of effort, to consider his ready force as less than 300,000, indeed only just over 290,000.

There was behind this, it is true, a reserve of irregulars such as I have described, but the spirit furnishing those irregulars was uncertain, and the yield of them patchy and heterogeneous. Perhaps a quarter of the country responded readily to the appeal which was to call up a national militia. But even upon the eve of the Waterloo campaign there were departments, such as the Orne, which had not compelled five per cent. of those called to join the colours, such as the Pas de Calais and the Gers, which had not furnished eight per cent., and at the very last moment, of every twenty-five men called, not fifteen had come.

Add to this that Napoleon must strike at once or not at all, and it will readily be seen how desperate his situation was. His great chiefs of the higher command were not united in his service, the issue was doubtful, and to join Napoleon was to be a rebel should he fail,—was to be a rebel, that is, in case of a very probable event. The marvel is that so many of the leading men who had anything to lose undertook the chances at all. Finally, even of the total force available to him at that early moment when he was compelled to strike, Napoleon could strike with but a fraction. Less than half of the men available could he gather to deliver this decisive blow; and that blow, be it remembered, he could deliver at but one of the various hosts which were preparing to advance against him.

He was thus handicapped by two things: first, the necessity under which he believed himself to be of leaving considerable numbers to watch the frontiers. Secondly, and most important, the limitations imposed upon him by his lack of provision. With every effort, he could not fully arm and equip and munition a larger force than that which he gathered in early June for his last desperate throw; and the body upon the immediate and decisive success of which everything depended numbered but 124,000 men.

With this force Napoleon proceeded to attack the Allies in the Netherlands. *There* was a belt of French-speaking population. *There* was that body of the Allies which lay nearest to his hand, and over which, if he were but victorious, his victory would have its fullest effect. *There* were the troops under Wellington, a defeat of which would mean the cutting off of England, the financier of the Allies, from the Continent. *There* was present a population many elements of which sympathised with him and with the French revolutionary effort. Finally, the allied force in Belgium was the least homogeneous of the forces with which he would have to deal in the long succession of struggle from which even a success at this moment would not spare him.

From all these causes combined, and for the further reason that Paris was most immediately threatened from this neighbouring Belgian frontier, it was upon that frontier that Napoleon determined to cast his spear. It was upon the 5th of June that the first order was sent out for the concentration of this army for the invasion of Belgium.

In ten days the 124,000 men, with their 370 guns, were massed upon the line between Maubeuge and Philippeville, immediately upon the frontier, and ready to cross it. The way in which the frontier was passed and the river Sambre crossed before the first actions took place form between them the preliminaries of the campaign, and must be the subject of my next section.

II

THE PRELIMINARIES: NAPOLEON'S ADVANCE ACROSS THE SAMBRE

To understand the battle of Waterloo it is necessary, more perhaps than in the case of any other great decisive action, to read it strategically: that is, to regard the final struggle of Sunday the 18th of June as only the climax of certain general movements, the first phase of which was the concentration of the French Army of the North, and the second the passage of the Sambre river and the attack. This second phase covered four days in time, and in space an advance of nearly forty miles.

There is a sense, of course, in which it is true of every battle that its result is closely connected with the strategy which led up to its tactical features: how the opposing forces arrived upon the field, in what condition, and in what disposition and at what time, with what advantage or disadvantage, is always necessarily connected with the history of the campaign rather than of the individual action; but, as we saw in the case of Blenheim, and as might be exemplified from a hundred other cases, the greater part of battles can be understood by following the tactical dispositions upon the field. They are won or lost, in the main, according to those dispositions.

With Waterloo it was not so. Waterloo was lost by Napoleon, won by the Allies, *not* mainly on account of tactical movements upon the field itself, but mainly on account of what had happened in the course of the advance of the French army to that field. In other words, the military character of that great decisive action is always missed by those who have read it isolated from the movements immediately preceding it.

Napoleon, determining to strike at Belgium under the political circumstances we have already seen, was attacking forces about double his own.

He was like one man coming up rapidly and almost unexpectedly to attack two: but hoping if possible to deal successively and singly with either opponent.

His doubtful chance of success in such a hazard obviously lay in his being able to attack each enemy separately: that is, to engage first one before the second came to his aid; then the second; and thus to defeat each in turn. The chance of victory under such circumstances is slight. It presupposes the surprise of the two allied adversaries by their single opponent, and the defeat of one so quickly that the other cannot come to his aid till all is over. But no other avenue of victory is open to a man fighting enemies of double his numerical strength; at least under conditions where armament, material, and racial type are much the same upon either side.

The possibility of dealing thus with his enemy Napoleon thought possible, and thought it possible from two factors in the situation before him.

The first factor was that the allied army, seeing its great numbers, the comparatively small accumulation of supplies which it could yet command, the great length of frontier which it had to watch, was spread out in a great number of cantonments, the whole stretch of which was no less than one hundred miles in length, from Liège upon the east or left to Tournay upon the west or right.

The second factor which gave Napoleon his chance was that this long line depended for its supply, its orders, its line of retreat upon two separate and opposite bases.

The left or eastern half, formed mainly of Prussian subjects, and acting under Blucher, had arrived from the east, looked for safety in case of defeat to a retreat towards the Rhine, obtained its supplies from that direction, and in general was fed from the *east* along those communications, continual activity along which are as necessary to the life of an army as the uninterrupted working of the air-tube is necessary to the life of a diver.

The western or right-hand part of the line, Dutch, German, Belgian, and British, acting under Wellington, depended, upon the contrary, upon the North Sea, and upon communication across that sea with England. That is, it drew its supplies and the necessaries of its existence from the *west*, the opposite and contrary direction from that to which the Prussian half of the Allies were looking for theirs. The effect of this upon the campaign is at once simple to perceive and of capital importance in Napoleon's plan.

Wellington and Blucher did not, under the circumstances, oppose to Napoleon a single body drawing its life from one stream of communications. They did not in combination command a force defending one goal; they commanded two forces defending two goals. The thorough defeat of one would throw it back away from the other if the attack were delivered at the point where the two just joined hands; and the English[1] or western half under Wellington was bound to movements actually contrary to the Prussian or eastern half under Blucher in case either were defeated before the other could come to its aid.

Napoleon, then, in his rapid advance upon Belgium, was a man conducting a column against a line. He was conducting that column against one special point, the point of junction between two disparate halves of an opposing line. He advanced therefore upon a narrow front perpendicular to, and aimed at the centre of, the long scattered cordon of his double enemy, which cordon it was his business if possible to divide just where the western end of one half touched the eastern end of the other. He designed to fight in detail

---

[1] I use the word "English" here to emphasise the character of Wellington's command; for though even this second half of the allied line was not in its majority of British origin, yet it contained a large proportion of British troops; the commander was an Englishman, the Duke of Wellington, and the best elements in the force were from these islands.

the first portion he could engage, then to turn upon the other, and thus to defeat both singly and in turn.

I will put this strategical position before the reader in the shape of an English parallel in order to make it the plainer, and I will then, by the aid of sketch maps, show how the Allies actually lay upon the Belgian frontier at the moment when Napoleon delivered his attack upon it.

Imagine near a quarter million of men spread out in a line of separate cantonments from Windsor at one extremity to Bristol at the other; and suppose that the eastern half of this line from Windsor to as far west as Wallingford is depending for its supplies and its communications upon the river Thames and its road system, and is prepared in case of defeat to fall back, down the valley of that stream towards London.

On the other hand, imagine that the western half from Swindon to Bristol is receiving its supplies from the Severn and the Bristol Channel, and must in case of defeat fall back westward upon that line.

Now, suppose an invading column rather more than 120,000 strong to be advancing from the south against this line, but prepared to strike up from almost any point on the Channel. It strikes, as a fact, from Southampton, and marches rapidly north by Winchester and Newbury. By the time it has reached Newbury, the eastern half of the opposing line, that between Wallingford and Windsor, has concentrated to meet it, but is defeated in the neighbourhood of that town.

Such a battle at Newbury would correspond to the battle at Ligny (let it be fought upon a Friday). Meanwhile, the western half, hurrying up in aid, has failed to effect a junction before the eastern half was defeated, comes up too late above Newbury, and finding it is too late, retires upon Abingdon. The victorious invader pursues them, and at noon on the second day engages them in a long line which they hold in front of Abingdon.

If he has only to deal in front of Abingdon with this second or western half, which hurried up too late to help the defeated eastern half, he has very fair chances of success. He is slightly superior numerically; he has, upon the whole, better troops and he has more guns. But the eastern half of the defending army, which has been beaten at Newbury, though beaten, was neither destroyed nor dispersed, nor thrust very far back from the line of operations. It has retreated to Wallingford, that is towards the north, parallel to the retreat of the western half; and a few hours after this western half is engaged in battle with the invader in front of Abingdon, the eastern half appears upon that invader's right flank, joins forces with the line of the defenders at Abingdon, and thus brings not only a crushing superiority of numbers upon the field against the invader, but also brings it up in such a manner that he is compelled to fight upon two fronts at once. He is, of course, destroyed by such a combination, and his army routed and dispersed. An action of this sort fought at Abingdon would correspond to the action which was fought upon the field of Waterloo, supposing, of course, for the purpose of this rough parallel, an open countryside without the obstacle of the river.

The actual positions of the two combined commands, the command of Blucher and the command of Wellington, which between them held the long line between Tournay and Liège, will be grasped from the sketch map upon the next page.

The reader who would grasp the campaign in the short compass of such an essay as this had best consider the numbers and the positions in a form not too detailed, and busy himself with a picture which, though accurate, shall be general.

Let him, then, consider the whole line between Liège and Tournay to consist of the two halves already presented: a western half, which we will call the Duke of Wellington's, and an eastern half, which we will call Blucher's: of these two the Duke of Wellington was Commander-in-chief.

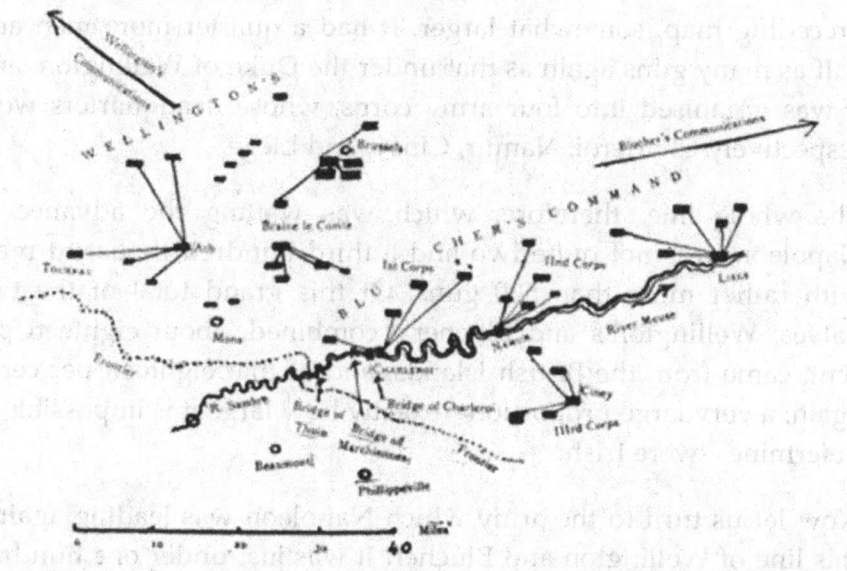

Next, note the numbers of each and their disposition. The mixed force under the Duke of Wellington was somewhat over 100,000 men, with just over 200 guns.[2] They consisted in two corps and a reserve. The first corps was under the Prince of Orange, and was mainly composed of men from the Netherlands. Its headquarters were at Braine le Comte. The second corps was under Lord Hill, and contained the mass of the British troops present. Its headquarters were at Ath. These two between them amounted to about half of Wellington's command, and we find them scattered in cantonments at Oudenarde, at Ath, at Enghien, at Soignies, at Nivelles, at Roeulx, at Braine le Comte, at Hal. A reserve corps under the Duke's own command was stationed at Brussels, and amounted to more than one-fifth, but less than one-quarter, of the whole force. The remaining quarter and a little more is accounted for by scattered cavalry (mainly in posts upon the river Dender), by the learned arms, gunners and sappers, distributed throughout the army, and by troops which were occupying garrisons—in numbers amounting to rather more than ten per cent of the force.

The eastern Prussian or left half of the line was, as is apparent in the

---

[2] Rather more than 106,000; guns 204.

preceding map, somewhat larger. It had a quarter more men and half as many guns again as that under the Duke of Wellington, and it was organised into four army corps, whose headquarters were respectively Charleroi, Namur, Ciney, and Liège.

The whole line, therefore, which was waiting the advance of Napoleon, was not quite two and a third hundred thousand men, with rather more than 500 guns. Of this grand total of the two halves, Wellington's and Blucher's combined, about eighteen per cent. came from the British Islands, and of that eighteen per cent., again, a very large proportion—exactly how large it is impossible to determine—were Irish.

Now let us turn to the army which Napoleon was leading against this line of Wellington and Blucher. It was just under one hundred and a quarter thousand men strong, that is, just over half the total number of its opponents. It had, however, a heavier proportion of guns, which were two-thirds as numerous as those it had to meet.

This "Army of the North" was organised in seven great bodies, unequal in size, but each a unit averaging seventeen odd thousand men. These seven great bodies were the 1st, 2nd, 3rd, 4th Army Corps, the 6th Army Corps, the Imperial Guard, and the reserve cavalry under Grouchy.

The concentration of this army began, as I said in a previous section, upon the 5th of June, and was effected with a rapidity and order which are rightly regarded as a model by all writers upon military science.

The French troops, when the order for concentration was given, stretched westward as far as Lille, eastward as far as Metz, southward as far as Paris, in the neighbourhood of which town was the Imperial Guard. The actual marching of the various units occupied a week. Napoleon was at the front on the night of the 13th of June; the whole army was upon the 14th drawn up upon a line stretched from Maubeuge to Philippeville, and the attack was ready to begin.

The concentration had been effected with singular secrecy, as well as with the promptitude and accuracy we have noted; and though the common opinion of Wellington and Blucher, that Napoleon had no intention of attacking, reposed upon sound general judgment—for the hazard Napoleon was playing in this game of one against two was extreme,—nevertheless it is remarkable that both of these great commanders should have been so singularly ignorant of the impending blow. Napoleon himself was actually over the frontier at the moment when Wellington was writing at his ease that he intended to take the offensive at the end of the month, and Blucher, a few days earlier, had expressed the opinion that he might be kept inactive for a whole year, since Bonaparte had no intention of attacking.

By the evening of Wednesday, June the 14th, all was ready for the advance, which was ordered for the next morning.

It would but confuse the general reader to attempt to carry with him through this short account the name and character of each commander, but it is essential to remember one at least—the name of *Erlon*; and he should also remember that the corps which Erlon commanded was the *First* Corps; for, as we shall see, upon Erlon's wanderings with this First Corps depended the unsatisfactory termination of Ligny, and the subsequent intervention of the Prussians at Waterloo, which decided that action.

It is also of little moment for the purpose of this to retain the names of the places which were the headquarters of each of these corps before the advance began. It is alone important to the reader that he should have a clear picture of the order in which this advance took place, for thus only will he understand both where it struck, and why, with all its rapidity, it suffered from certain shocks or jerks.

Napoleon's advance was upon three parallel lines and in three main bodies.

The left or westernmost consisted of the First and Second Corps d'Armée; the centre, of the Imperial Guard, together with the Third and Sixth Corps. The third or right consisted of the Fourth Corps alone, with a division of cavalry. These three bodies, when the night of Wednesday the 14th of June fell, lay, the first at Sorle and Leer; the second at Beaumont, and upon the road that runs through it to Charleroi; the third at Philippeville.

It is at this stage advisable to consider why Napoleon had chosen the crossing of the Sambre at Charleroi and the sites immediately to the north on the left bank of that river as the point where he would strike at the long line of the Allies.

Many considerations converged to impose this line of advance upon Napoleon. In the first place, it was his task to cut the line of the Allies in two at the point where the extremity of one army, the Prussian, touched upon the extremity of the other, that of the Duke of Wellington. This point lay due north of the river-crossing he had chosen.

Again, the main road to Brussels was barred by the fortress of Mons, which, though not formidable, had been put in some sort of state of defence.

Again, as a glance at the accompanying map will show, the Prussian half of the allied line was drawn somewhat in front of the other half; and if Napoleon were to attack the enemy in detail, he must strike at the Prussians first. Finally, the line Maubeuge-Philippeville, upon which he concentrated his front, was, upon the whole, the most central position in the long line of his frontier troops, which stretched from Metz to the neighbourhood of the Straits of Dover. Being the most central point, not only with regard to these two extremities, but also with regard to distant Paris, it was the point upon which his concentration could most rapidly be effected.

This, then, was the position upon the night of the 14th. The three great bodies of French troops (much the largest of which was that in the centre) to march at dawn, the light cavalry moving as early as half past two, ahead of the centre, the whole body of which was to march on Charleroi.

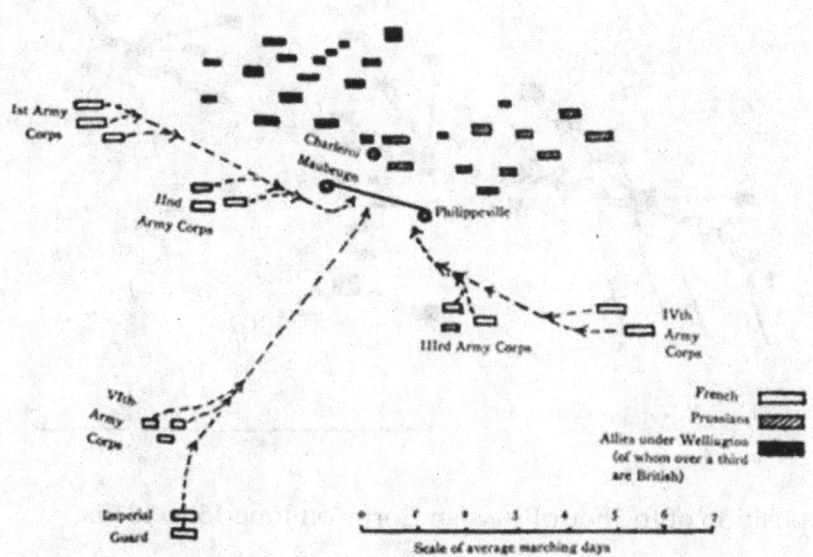

The left, that is the First and Second Corps, to cross the Sambre at Thuin, the Abbaye d'Aulne, and Marchiennes. (There were bridges at all three places.) The right or Fourth Corps was also to march on Charleroi.[3]

Napoleon intended to be over the river with all his men by the afternoon of the 15th, but, as we shall see, this "bunching" of fully half the advance upon one crossing place caused, not a fatal, but a prejudicial delay. Among other elements in this false calculation was an apparent error on the part of Soult, who blundered in some way which kept the Third Corps with the centre instead of relieving

---

[3] Surely an error in judgment, for thus the whole mass of the army, all of it except the First and Second Corps, would be crossing the Sambre at that one place, with all the delay such a plan would involve. As a fact, the Fourth Corps, or right wing of the advance, was at last sent over the river by Châtelet, but it would have been better to have given such orders at the beginning.

the pressure by sending it over with the Fourth to cross, under the revised instructions, by Châtelet.

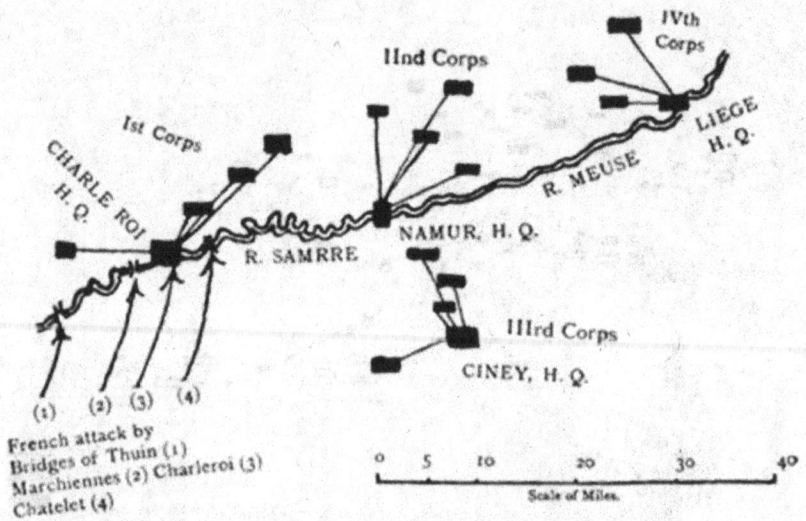

Disposition of the Four Prussian Corps on June 15th, 1815.

At dawn, then, the whole front of the French army was moving. It was the dawn of Thursday the 15th of June. By sunset of Sunday all was to be decided.

At this point it is essential to grasp the general scheme of the operations which are about to follow.

Put in its simplest elements and graphically, the whole business began in some such form as is presented in the accompanying sketch map.

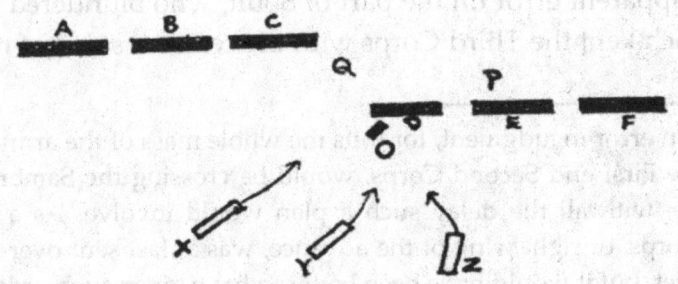

Napoleon's advancing army X Y Z, marching on Thursday, June 15th, strikes at O (which is Charleroi), the centre of the hundred-mile-long line of cantonments A B C— —D E F, which form the two armies of the Allies, twice as numerous as his own, but thus dispersed. Just behind Charleroi (O) are a hamlet and a village, called respectively Quatre Bras (Q) and Ligny (P).

Napoleon succeeds in bringing the eastern or Prussian half of this long line D E F to battle and defeating it at Ligny (P) upon the next day, Friday, June 16th, before the western half, or Wellington's A B C, can come up in aid; and on the same day a portion of his forces, X, under his lieutenant, Marshal Ney, holds up that western half, just as it is attempting to effect its junction with the eastern half at Quatre Bras (Q), a few miles off from Ligny (P). The situation on the night of Friday, June 16th, at the end of this second step, is that represented in this second sketch map.

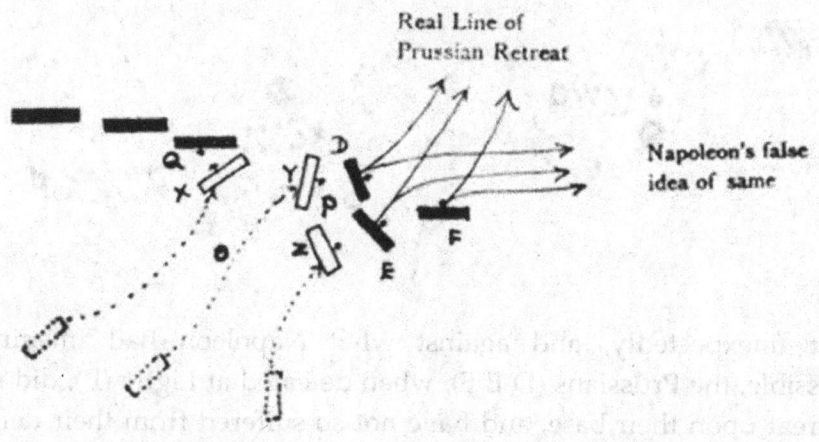

Believing the Prussians (D E F) to be retreating from Ligny towards their base eastward, and not northwards, Napoleon more or less neglects them and concentrates his main body in order to follow up Wellington's western half (A B C), and in the hope of defeating *that* in its turn, as he has already defeated the eastern or Prussian half (D E F) at Ligny (P). With this object Napoleon advances northward during all the third day, Saturday, June 17th. Wellington (A B C) retreats north before him during that same day, and then, on the morrow, the 18th, Sunday, turns to give battle at Waterloo (W). Napoleon engages him with fair chances of success, and the situation as the battle begins at midday on the 18th is that sketched in this third map.

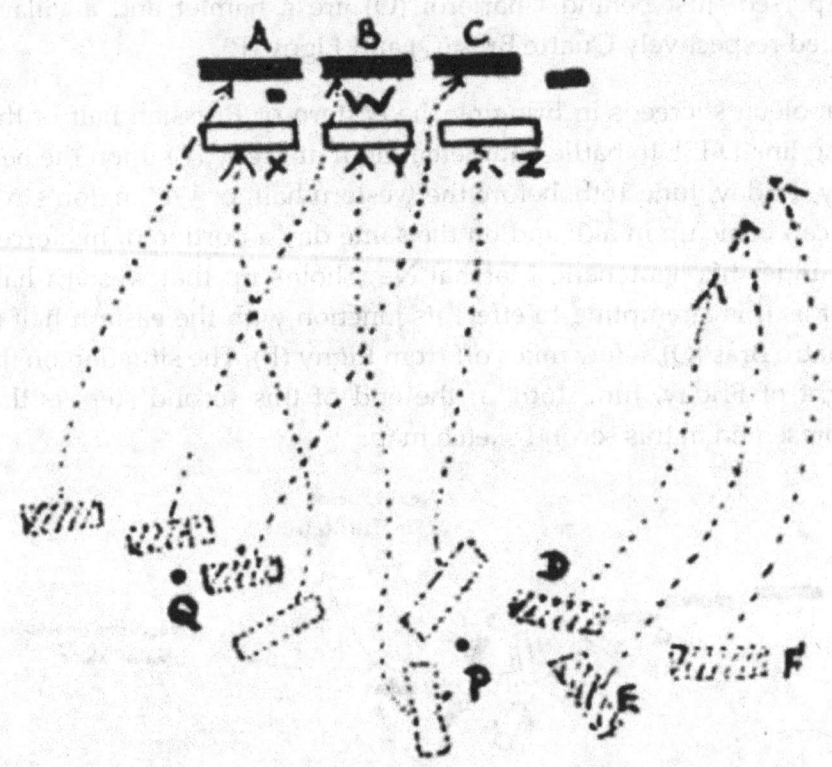

But unexpectedly, and against what Napoleon had imagined possible, the Prussians (D E F), when defeated at Ligny (P), did not retreat upon their base, and have not so suffered from their defeat as to be incapable of further action. They have marched northward parallel to the retreat of Wellington; and while Napoleon (X Y Z) is at the hottest of his struggle with Wellington (A B C) at Waterloo (W), this eastern or Prussian half (D E F) comes down upon his flank at (R) in the middle of the afternoon, and by the combined numbers and disposition of this double attack Napoleon's army is crushed before darkness sets in.

Such, in its briefest graphic elements, is the story of the four days.

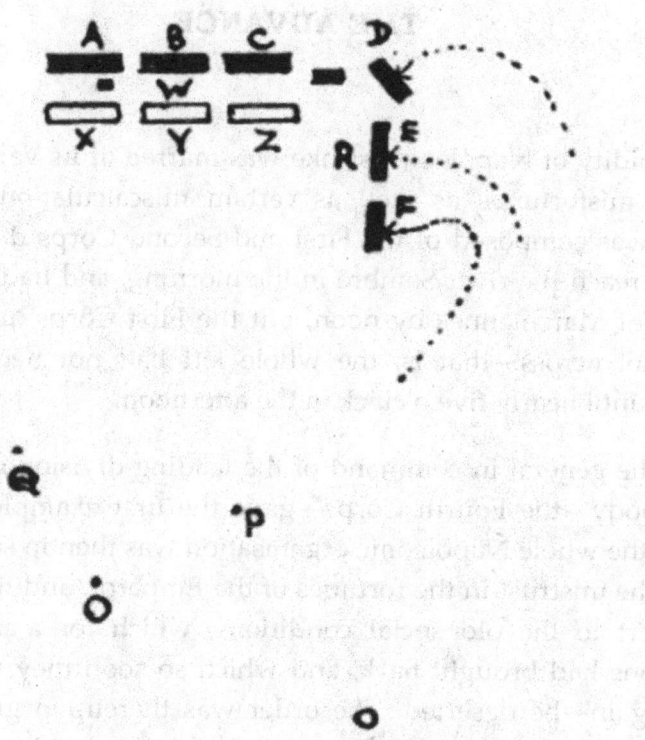

It will be observed from what we have said that the whole thing turns upon the incompleteness of Napoleon's success at Ligny, and the power of *retreating northward* left to the Prussians after that defeat.

When we come to study the details of the story, we shall see that this, the Prussian defeat at Ligny, was thus incomplete because one of Napoleon's subordinates, Erlon, with the First French Army Corps, received contradictory orders and did not come up as he should have done to turn the battle of Ligny into a decisive victory for Napoleon. A part of Napoleon's forces being thus neutralised and held useless during the fight at Ligny, the Prussian army escaped, still formed as a fighting force, and still capable of reappearing, as it did reappear, at the critical moment, two days later, upon the field of Waterloo.

THE ADVANCE

The rapidity of Napoleon's stroke was marred at its very outset by certain misfortunes as well as certain miscalculations. His left, which was composed of the First and Second Corps d'Armée, did indeed reach the river Sambre in the morning, and had carried the bridge of Marchiennes by noon, but the First Corps, under Erlon, were not across—that is, the whole left had not negotiated the river—until nearly five o'clock in the afternoon.

Next, the general in command of the leading division of the right-hand body—the Fourth Corps—gave the first example of that of which the whole Napoleonic organisation was then in such terror, I mean the mistrust in the fortunes of the Emperor, and the tendency to revert to the old social conditions, which for a moment the Bourbons had brought back, and which so soon they might bring back again—he deserted. The order was thereupon given for the Fourth Corps or right wing to cross at Châtelet, but it came late (as late as half-past three in the afternoon), and did but cause delay. At this eastern end of Napoleon's front the last men were not over the river until the next day.

As to the centre (the main body of the army), its cavalry reached Charleroi before ten o'clock in the morning, but an unfortunate and exasperating accident befallen a messenger left the infantry immediately behind without instructions. The cavalry were impotent to force the bridge crossing the river Sambre, which runs through the town, until the main body should appear, and it was not until past noon that the main body began crossing the Sambre by the Charleroi bridge. The Emperor had probably intended to fight immediately after having crossed the river. Gosselies, to the north, was strongly held; and had all his men been over the Sambre in the early afternoon as he had intended, an action fought suddenly, by surprise as it were, against the advance bodies of the First Prussian Corps, would have given the first example of that destruction of the enemy in detail which Napoleon intended. But the delays in the advance, rapid as it had been, now forbade any such good fortune. The end of the daylight was spent in pushing back the head of the First Prussian Corps (with a loss of somewhat over 1000 men), and when night fell upon that Thursday evening, the 15th of June, the French held Charleroi and all the crossings of the Sambre, but were not yet in a position to attack in force. Of the left, the First Corps were but just over the Sambre; on the right, that is, of the Fourth Corps, some units were still upon the other side of the river; while, of the centre, the *whole* of the Sixth Corps, and a certain proportion of cavalry as well, had still to cross!

Napoleon had failed to bring the enemy to action; that enemy had fallen back upon Fleurus, pretty nearly intact.[4] All the real work had evidently to be put off, not only until the morrow, but until a fairly late hour upon the morrow, for it would take some time to get all the French forces on to the Belgian side of the river.

When this should have been accomplished, however, the task of the next day, the Friday, was clear.

It was Napoleon's business to fall upon whatever Prussian force might be concentrated before him and upon his right and to destroy it, meanwhile holding back, by a force sent up the Brussels road to Quatre Bras, any attempt Wellington and his western army might make to join the Prussians and save them.

That night the Duke of Wellington's army lay in its cantonments without concentration and without alarm, guessing nothing. The head of Wellington's First Corps, the young Prince of Orange, who commanded the Netherlanders, had left his headquarters to go and dine with the Duke in Brussels.

Wellington, we may believe if we choose (the point is by no means certain), knew as early as three o'clock in the afternoon that the French had moved. It may have been as late as five, it may even

---

[4] There were some five hundred Prussian prisoners.

have been six. But whatever the hour in which he received his information, it is quite certain that he had no conception of the gravity of the moment. As late as ten o'clock at night the Duke issued certain after-orders. He had previously given general orders (which presupposed no immediate attack), commanding movements which would in the long-run have produced a concentration, but though these orders were ordered to be executed "with as little delay as possible," there was no hint of immediate duty required, nor do the posts indicated betray in any way the urgent need there was to push men south and east at the top of their speed, and relieve the Prussians from the shock they were to receive on the morrow.

These general orders given—orders that betray no grasp of the nearness of the issue—Wellington went off to the Duchess of Richmond's ball in what the impartial historian cannot doubt to be ignorance of the great stroke which Napoleon had so nearly brought off upon that very day, and would certainly attempt to bring off upon the next.

In the midst of the ball, or rather during the supper, definite news came in that the French army had crossed the river Sambre, and had even pushed its cavalry as far up the Brussels road as Quatre Bras.

The Duke does not seem to have appreciated even then what that should mean in the way of danger to the Prussians, and indeed of the breaking of the whole line. He left the dance at about two in the morning and went to bed.

He was not long left in repose. In the bright morning sunlight, four hours afterwards, he was roused by a visitor from the frontier, and we have it upon his evidence that the Duke at last understood what was before him, and said that the concentration of his forces must be at Quatre Bras.

In other words, Wellington knew or appreciated extremely tardily on that *Friday* morning about six that the blow was about to fall upon his Prussian allies to the south and east, and that it was the business of his army upon the west to come up rapidly in succour.

As will be seen in a moment, he failed; but it would be a very puerile judgment of this great man and superb defensive General to belittle his place in the history of war upon the basis of even such errors as these.

True, the error and the delay were prodigious and, in a fashion, comic; and had Napoleon delivered upon the *Thursday* afternoon, as he had intended, an attack which should have defeated the Prussians before him, Wellington's error and delay would have paid a very heavy price.

As it was, Napoleon's own delay in crossing the Sambre made Wellington's mistake and tardiness bear no disastrous fruit. The Duke failed to succour the Prussians. His troops, scattered all over Western Belgium, did not come up in time to prevent the defeat of his allies at Ligny. But he held his own at Quatre Bras; and in the final battle, forty-eight hours later, the genius with which he handled his raw troops upon the ridge of Mont St Jean wiped out and negatived all his strategical misconceptions of the previous days.

From this confusion, this partial delay and error upon Napoleon's part, this ignorance upon Wellington's of what was toward, both of which marked Thursday the 15th, we must turn to a detailed description of that morrow, Friday the 16th, which, though it is less remembered in history than the crowning day of Waterloo, was, in every military sense, the decisive day of the campaign.

We shall see that it was Napoleon's failure upon that Friday completely to defeat, or rather to destroy, the Prussian force at Ligny—a failure largely due to Wellington's neighbouring resistance at Quatre Bras—which determined the Emperor's final defeat upon the Sunday at Waterloo.

III

THE DECISIVE DAY

Friday the 16th of June

Quatre Bras and Ligny

We have seen what the 15th of June was in those four short days of which Waterloo was to be the climax. That Thursday was filled with an advance, rapid and unexpected, against the centre of the allied line, and therefore against that weak point where the two halves of the allied line joined, to wit, Charleroi and the country immediately to the north of that town and bridge.

We have further seen that while the unexpectedness of the blow was almost as thorough as Napoleon could have wished, the rapidity of its delivery, though considerable, had been less than he had anticipated. He had got by the evening of the day not much more than three-quarters of his forces across the river Sambre, and this passage, which was mapped out for completion before nightfall, straggled on through the whole morning of the morrow,—a tardiness the effects of which we shall clearly see in the next few pages.

Napoleon's intention, once the Sambre was crossed, was to divide his army into two bodies: one, on the left, was to be entrusted to Ney; one, on the right, to Grouchy. A reserve, which the Emperor would command in person, was to consist in the main of the Imperial Guard.

The left-hand body, under Ney, was to go straight north up the great Brussels road.

Napoleon rightly estimated that he had surprised the foe, though he exaggerated the extent of that surprise. He thought it possible that this body to the left, under Ney, might push on to Brussels itself, and in any case could easily deal with the small and unprepared forces which it might meet upon the way. Its function in any case, whether resistance proved slight or formidable, was to hold the forces of Wellington back from effecting a junction with Blucher and the Prussians.

Meanwhile, the right-hand body, under Grouchy, was to fall upon the extremity of the Prussian line and overwhelm it.

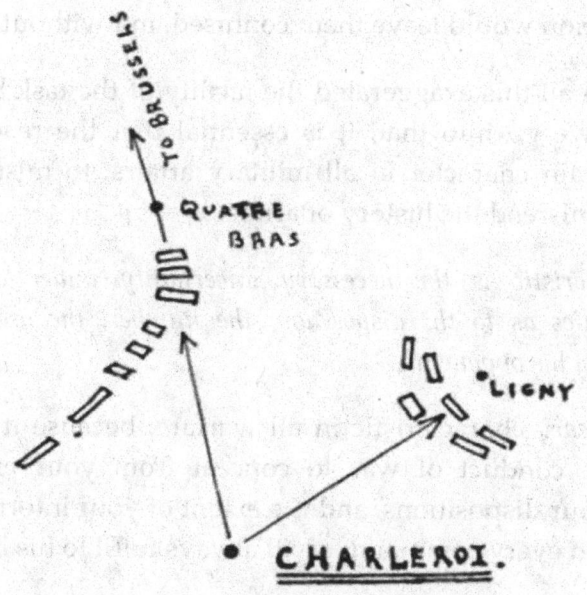

Such an action against the head of the long Prussian cordon could lead, as the Emperor thought, to but one of two results: either the great majority of the Prussian force, coming up to retrieve this first disaster, would be defeated in detail as it came; or, more probably, finding itself cut off from all aid on the part of Wellington's forces to the west and its head crushed, the long Prussian line would roll up backwards upon its communications towards the east, whence it had come.

In either case the prime object of Napoleon's sudden move would have been achieved; and, with the body upon the left, under Ney, pushing up the Brussels road, the body upon the right, under Grouchy, pushing back the head of the Prussian line eastward, the two halves of the Allies would be separated altogether, and could later be dealt with, each in turn. The capital disadvantage under which Napoleon suffered—the fact that he had little more than half as many men as his combined enemies—would be neutralised, because he would, after the separation of those enemies into two bodies, be free to deal with either at his choice. Their communications came from diametrically opposite directions,[5] and, as the plan of each depended upon the co-operation of the other, their separation would leave them confused and without a scheme.

Napoleon in all this exaggerated the facility of the task before him; but before we go into that, it is essential that the reader should grasp a certain character in all military affairs, to misunderstand which is to misread the history of armies.

This characteristic is the necessary uncertainty under which every commander lies as to the disposition, the number, the order, and the information of his opponents.

It is a *necessary* characteristic in all warfare, because it is a prime duty in the conduct of war to conceal from your enemy your numbers, your dispositions, and the extent of your information. It is a duty which every commander will always fulfil to his best ability.

It is therefore a characteristic, be it noted, which no development of human science can conceivably destroy, for with every advance in our means of communicating information we advance also in our knowledge of the means whereby the new means of communication may be interrupted. An advantage over the enemy in the means one has of acquiring knowledge with regard to him must, of course, always be of supreme importance, and when those means are novel, one side or the other is often beforehand for some years with the new science of their use. When such is the case,

---

[5] See ante, pp. 11 and 15.

science appears to uninstructed opinion to have changed this ancient and fixed characteristic which is in the very nature of war. But in fact there has been no such change. Under the most primitive conditions an advantage of this type was of supreme importance; under conditions the most scientific and refined it is an advantage that may still be neutralised if the enemy has learnt means of screening himself as excellent as our means of discovering him. Even the aeroplane, whose development in the modern French service has so vastly changed the character of information, and therefore of war, can never eliminate the factor of which I speak. A service possessed of a great superiority in this new arm will, of course, be the master of its foe; but when the use of the new arm is spread and equalised among all European forces so that two opposing forces are equally matched even in this new discovery, then the old element of move and countermove, feint, secrecy, and calculated confusion of an adversary, will reappear.[6]

In general, then, to point out the ignorance and the misconceptions of one commander is no criticism of a campaign until we have appreciated the corresponding ignorance and misconceptions of the other. We have already seen Wellington taken almost wholly by surprise on the French advance; we shall see him, even when he appreciated its existence, imagining it to be directed principally against himself. We shall similarly see Napoleon underestimating the Prussian force in front of him, and underestimating even that tardy information which had reached Wellington in time for him to send troops up the Brussels road, and to check the French advance along it. But we must judge either of the two great opponents not by a single picture of his own misconceptions alone, but by the combined picture of the misconceptions of both, and especially by a

---

[6] A lengthy digression might here be admitted upon the question of how defence against aerial scouting will develop. That it will develop none can doubt. Every such advantage upon the part of one combatant has at last been neutralised by the spread of a common knowledge and a common method to all.

consideration of the way in which each retrieved or attempted to retrieve the results of those misconceptions when a true idea of the enemy's dispositions was conveyed to him.

Here, then, we have Napoleon on the morning of Friday the 16th of June prepared to deal with the Prussians. It is his right-hand body, under Grouchy, which is deputed to do this, while he sends up the left-hand body, under Ney, northwards to brush aside, or, at the worst, at least to hold off whatever of the Duke of Wellington's command may be found upon the Brussels road attempting to join the Prussians.

The general plan of what happened upon that decisive 16th is simple enough.

The left-hand body, under Ney, goes forward up the Brussels road, finds more resistance than it expected, but on the whole performs its task and prevents any effective help being given by the western half of the Allies—Wellington's half—to the eastern half—the Prussian half. But it only prevents that task with difficulty and at the expense of a tactical defeat. This action is called Quatre Bras.

Meanwhile, the right-hand body equally accomplishes the elements of its task, engages the head of the Prussian line and defeats it, with extreme difficulty, just before dark. This action is called Ligny.

But the minor business conducted by the left, under Ney, is only just successful, and successful only in the sense that it does, at vast expense, prevent a junction of Wellington with Blucher. The major business conducted on the right, by Napoleon himself, in support of Grouchy, is disappointing. The head of the Prussian line is not destroyed; the Prussian army, though beaten, is free to retreat in fair order, and almost in what direction it chooses.

The ultimate result is that Wellington and Blucher do manage to effect their junction on the day after the morrow of Ligny and Quatre Bras, and thus defeat Napoleon at Waterloo.

Now, why were both these operations, Quatre Bras and Ligny,

incompletely successful? Partly because there was more resistance along the Brussels road than Napoleon had expected, and a far larger body of Prussians in front of him than he had expected either; *but much more because a whole French army corps, which, had it been in action, could have added a third to the force of either the right or the left wing, was out of action all day; and wandered aimlessly over the empty zone which separated Ney from Grouchy, Quatre Bras from Ligny, the left half of Napoleon's divided army from its right half.*

This it was which prevented what might have been possible—the thrusting back of Wellington along the Brussels road, and even perhaps the disorganisation of his forces. This it was which missed what was otherwise certainly possible—the total ruin of the Prussian army.

This army corps thus thrown away unused in hours of aimless marching and countermarching was the First Army Corps. Its commander was Erlon; and the enormous blunder or fatality which permitted Erlon and his 20,000 to be as useless upon the 16th of June as though they had been wiped out in some defeat is what makes of the 16th of June the decisive day of the campaign.

It was Erlon's failure to be present *either* with Ney *or* with Grouchy, either upon the left or upon the right, either at Quatre Bras or at Ligny, while each of those two actions were in doubt, which made it possible for Wellington's troops to stand undefeated in the west, for the Prussians to retire—not intact, but still an army—from the east, and for both to unite upon the day after the morrow, the Sunday, and destroy the French army at Waterloo.

It is upon Erlon's blunder or misfortune that the whole issue turns, and upon the Friday, the 16th of June, in the empty fields between Quatre-Bras and Ligny, much more than upon the famous Sunday at Waterloo, that the fate of Napoleon's army was decided.

In order to make this clear, let us first follow what happened in the operations of Napoleon's right wing against the Prussians opposed to it,—operations which bear in history the name of "the Battle of Ligny."

LIGNY

"If they fight here they will be damnably mauled."
(Wellington's words on seeing the defensive positions chosen by the Prussians at Ligny.)

Napoleon imagined that when he had crossed the Sambre with the bulk of his force, the suddenness of his attack (for, though retarded as we have seen, and though leaving troops upon the wrong bank of the river, it was sudden) would find the Prussian forces in the original positions wherein he knew them to have lain before he marched. He did not think that they would yet have had the time, still less the intention, to concentrate. Those original positions the map upon p. 19 makes plain.

The 124,000 men and more, which lay under the supreme command of Blucher, had been spread before the attack began along the whole extended line from Liège to Charleroi, and had been disposed regularly from left to right in four corps d'armée.

The first of these had its headquarters in Charleroi itself, its furthest outpost was but five miles east of the town, its three brigades had Charleroi for their centre; its reserve cavalry was at Sombreffe, its reserve artillery at Gembloux. The Second Corps had its headquarters twenty miles away east, at Namur, and occupied posts in the country as far off as Hannut (thirty miles away from Charleroi).

The Third Corps had its headquarters at Ciney in the Ardennes, and was scattered in various posts throughout that forest, its furthest cantonment being no nearer than Dinant, which, by the only good road available, was nearer forty than thirty miles from Napoleon's point of attack.

Finally, the Fourth Corps was as far away as Liège (nearer fifty than forty miles by road from the last cantonment of the First Corps), and having its various units scattered round the neighbourhood of that town.

Napoleon, therefore, attacking Charleroi suddenly, imagined that he would have to deal only with the First Corps at Charleroi and its neighbourhood. He did not think that the other three corps had information in time to enable them to come up westward towards the end of the line and meet him. The outposts of the First Corps had, of course, fallen back before the advance of the Emperor's great army; the mass of that First Corps was, he knew, upon this morning of the 16th, some mile or two north and east of Fleurus, astraddle of the great road which leads from Charleroi to Gembloux. At the very most, and supposing this First Corps (which was of 33,000 men, under Ziethen) had received reinforcements from the nearest posts of the Second and the Third Corps, Napoleon did not think that he could have in front of him more than some 40,000 men at the most.

He was in error. It had been arranged among the Prussian leaders that resistance to Napoleon, when occasion might come for it, should be offered in the neighbourhood of the cross-roads where the route from Charleroi to Gembloux crosses that from Nivelles to Namur. In other words, they were prepared to stand and fight between Sombreffe and the village of Ligny. The plan had been prepared long beforehand. The whole of the First Corps was in position with the morning, awaiting the Emperor's attack. The Second Corps had been in motion for hours, and was marching up during all that morning. So was the Third Corps behind it. Blucher himself had arrived upon the field of battle the day before (the 15th), and had written thence to his sovereign to say that he was fully prepared for action the next day.

Indeed, Blucher on the 15th confidently expected victory, and the end of the campaign then and there. He had a right to do so, for Napoleon's advance had been met by so rapid a concentration that, a little after noon on that Friday the 16th, and before the first shots were fired, well over 80,000 men were drawn up to receive the shock of Napoleon's right wing. But that right wing all told, even when the belated French troops beyond the Sambre had finally crossed that river, and even when the Emperor had brought up the Guard and the reserve, numbered but 63,000. Supposing the French had been able to use every man, which they were not, they counted but seven to nine of their opponents. And the nine were upon the defensive; the seven had to undertake the task of an assault.

It was late in the day before battle was joined. Napoleon had reached Fleurus at about ten o'clock in the morning, but it was four hours more before he had brought all his troops across the river, and by the time he had done so two things had happened. First, the Duke of Wellington (who, as we shall see later, had come to Quatre Bras that morning, and had written to Blucher telling him of his arrival) rode off in person to the Prussian positions and discussed affairs near the windmill of Bussy with the Prussian Commander-in-chief. In this conversation, Wellington undoubtedly promised to effect, if he could, a junction with the Prussians in the course of the afternoon. Even without that aid Blucher felt fairly sure of victory; with it, he could be perfectly confident.

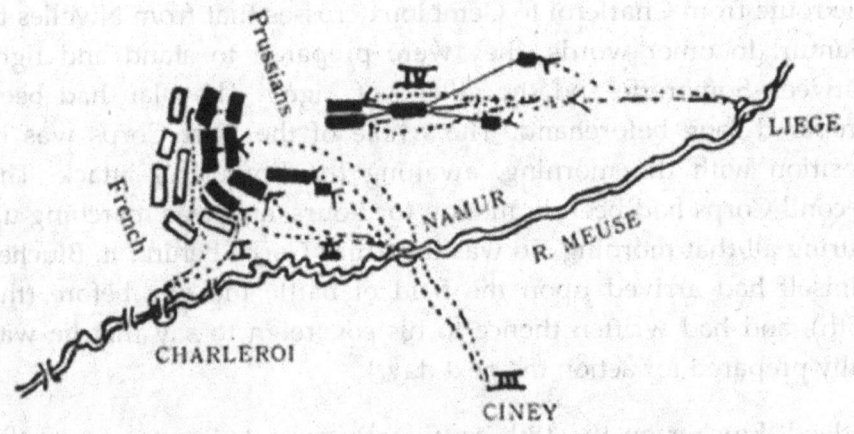

The Prussian concentration before Ligny, showing the junction of the First, Second, and Third Corps on the morning of June 16th, and the inability of the Fourth Corps to come up in time.

As matters turned out, Wellington found himself unable to effect his junction with Blucher. Ney, as we shall see later, found in front of him on the Brussels road much heavier opposition than he had imagined, but Wellington was also surprised to find to what strength the French force under Ney was at Quatre Bras. Wellington, as we shall see, held his own on that 16th of June, but was quite unable to come up in succour of Blucher when the expected victory of that general turned to a defeat.

The second thing that happened in those hours was Napoleon's discovery that the Prussian troops massing to oppose him before Ligny were going to be much more than a single corps. It looked to him more like the whole Prussian army. It was, indeed, three-quarters of that army, for it consisted of the First, the Second, and the Third Corps. Only the Fourth, with its headquarters at distant Liège, had not been able to arrive in time. This Fourth Corps would also have been present, and would probably have turned the scale in favour of the Prussians, had the staff orders been sent out promptly and conveyed with sufficient rapidity. As it was, its most advanced units got no further west, during the course of the action, than about halfway between Liège and the battlefield.

Napoleon was enabled to discover with some ease the great numbers which had concentrated to oppose him from the fact that these numbers had concentrated upon a defective position. Wellington, the greatest defensive general of his time, at once discovered this weakness in Blucher's chosen battlefield, and was provoked by the discovery to the exclamation which stands at the head of this section. The rolling land occupied by the Prussian army lay exposed in a regular sweep downwards towards the heights upon which lay the French, and the Prussian army as it deployed came wholly under the view of its enemy. Nothing was hidden; and a further effect was that, as Napoleon himself remarked, all the artillery work of the French side went home. If a round missed the foremost positions of the Prussian army, it would necessarily fall within the ranks behind them.

This discovery, that there lay before him not one corps but a whole army, seemed to Napoleon, upon one condition, an advantage. The new development would, upon that one condition, give him, if his troops were of the quality he estimated them to be, a complete victory over the united Prussian force, and might well terminate the campaign on that afternoon and in that place. That one condition was the possibility of getting Ney upon the left, or some part at least of Ney's force, to leave the task of holding off Wellington, to come down upon the flank of the Prussians from the north and west, to envelop them, and thus, in company with the troops of Napoleon himself, to destroy the three Prussian Army Corps altogether.

Had that condition been fulfilled, the campaign would indeed have come to an end decisively in Napoleon's favour, and, as he put it in a famous phrase, "not a gun" of the army opposing him "should escape."

Unfortunately for the Emperor, that one condition was not fulfilled. The 63,000 Frenchmen of the right wing, under Napoleon, did indeed defeat and drive off the 80,000 men opposed to them. But that opposing army was not destroyed; it was not contained; it remained organised for further fighting, and it survived to decide Waterloo.

In order to appreciate Napoleon's idea and how it might have succeeded, let the reader consider the dispositions of the battle of Ligny.

The battlefield named in history after the village of Ligny consists of a number of communes, of which that village is the central one. The Prussian army held the villages marked on the map by the names of Tongrinelle and Tongrinne, to the east of Ligny; it held Brye, St Amand, and Wagnelée to the east. It held also the heights behind upon the great road leading from Nivelles to Namur. When Napoleon had at last got his latest troops over from beyond the Sambre on to the field of battle, which was not until just on two o'clock in the afternoon, the plan he formed was to hold the Prussian left and centre by a vigorous attack, that is, to pin the Prussians down to Tongrinne, Tongrinelle, and Ligny, while, on the other front, the east and south front of the Prussians, another vigorous attack should be driving them back out of Wagnelée and St Amand.

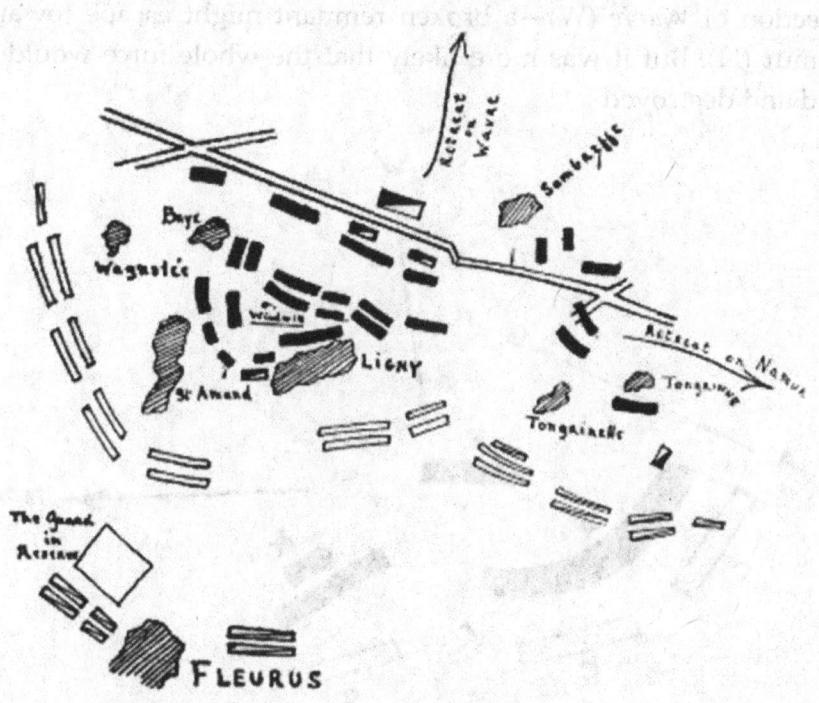

The plan can be further elucidated by considering the elements of the battle as they are sketched in the map over leaf. Napoleon's troops at C C C were to hold the Prussian left at H, to attack the Prussian right at D, with the Guard at E left in reserve for the final effort.

By thus holding the Prussians at H and pushing them in at D, he would here begin to pen them back, and it needed but the arrival on the field of a fresh French force attacking the Prussians along A B to destroy the force so contained and hemmed in. For that fresh force Napoleon depended upon new and changed instructions which he despatched to Ney when he saw the size of the Prussian force before him. During Napoleon's main attack, some portion of Ney's force, and if possible the whole of it, should appear unexpectedly from the north and west, marching down across the fields between Wagnelée and the Nivelles-Namur road, and coming on the north of the enemy at A B, so as to attack him not only in the flank but in the rear. He would then be unable to retreat in the direction of *Wavre* (W)—a broken remnant might escape towards Namur (N). But it was more likely that the whole force would be held and destroyed.

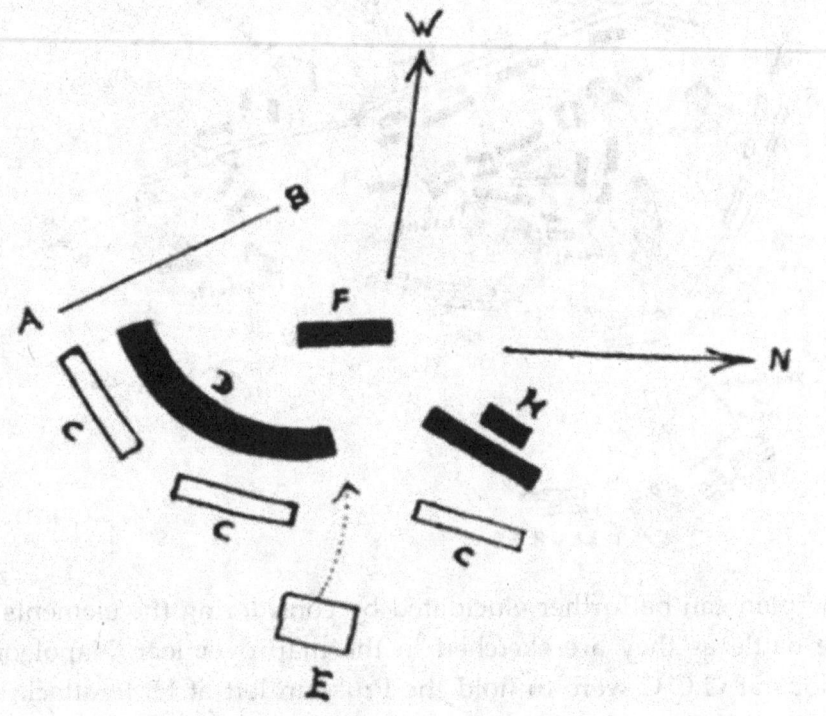

Elements of Ligny

Supposing that Napoleon's 63,000 showed themselves capable of holding, let alone partially driving in, the 80,000 in front of them, the sudden and unexpected appearance of a new force in the height of the action, adding another twenty or thirty thousand to the French troops already engaged, coming upon the flank and spreading to the rear of the Prussian host, would inevitably have destroyed that host, and, to repeat Napoleon's famous exclamation, "not a gun would have escaped."

The reader may ask: "If this plan of victory be so obvious, why did Napoleon send Ney off with a separate left wing of forty to fifty thousand men towards Quatre Bras?"

The answer is: that when, upon the day before, the Thursday, Napoleon had made this disposition, and given it as the general orders for that Friday, he had imagined only one corps of Prussians to be before him.

The right wing, with which the Emperor himself stayed, numbering, as we have seen, about 63,000 men, would have been quite enough to deal with that one Prussian corps; and he had sent so large a force, under Ney, up the Brussels road, not because he believed it would meet with serious opposition, but because this was to be the line of his principal advance, and it was his intention to occupy the town of Brussels at the very first opportunity. Having dealt with the single Prussian corps, as he had first believed it would be, in front of Fleurus, he meant that same evening to come back in person to the Brussels road and, in company with Ney, to conduct decisive operations against Wellington's half of the Allies, which would then, of course, be hopelessly outnumbered.

But when Napoleon saw, a little after midday of the Friday, that he had to deal with nearly the whole of the Prussian army, he perceived that the great force under Ney would be wasted out there on the west—supposing it to be meeting with little opposition—and had far better be used in deciding a crushing victory over the Prussians. To secure such a victory would, without bothering about the Duke of Wellington's forces to the westward, be quite enough to determine the campaign in favour of the French.

As early as two o'clock a note was sent to Ney urging him, when he had brushed aside such slight resistance as the Emperor expected him to find upon the Brussels road, to return and help to envelop the Prussian forces, which the Emperor was about to attack. At that hour it was not yet quite clear to Napoleon how large the Prussian force really was. This first note to Ney, therefore, was unfortunately not as vigorous as it might have been; though, even if it had been as vigorous as possible, Ney, who had found unexpected resistance upon the Brussels road, could certainly not have come up to help Napoleon with his whole force. He might, however, have spared a portion of it, and that portion, as we shall see later, would have been most obviously Erlon's corps—the First. Rather more than an hour later, at about a quarter-past three, when Napoleon had just joined battle with the Prussians, he got a note from Ney informing him that the left wing was meeting with considerable resistance, and could hardly abandon the place where it was engaged before Quatre Bras to come up against the Prussian flank at Ligny. Napoleon sent a note back to say that, none the less, an effort must be made at all costs to send Ney's forces to come over to him to attack the Prussian flank, for such an attack would mean the winning of a great decisive battle.

The distance over which these notes had to be carried to and fro, from Napoleon to Ney, was not quite five miles. The Emperor might therefore fairly expect after his last message that in the late middle of the afternoon—say half-past five or six—troops would appear upon his north-west horizon and march down to his aid. In good time such troops did appear; how inconclusively it will be my business to record.

Meanwhile, Napoleon had begun the fight at Ligny with his usual signal of three cannonshots, and between three and four o'clock the front of the whole army was engaged. It was for many hours mere hammer-and-tongs fighting, the French making little impression upon their right against Ligny or the villages to the east of it, but fighting desperately for St Amand and for Wagnelée. Such a course was part of Napoleon's plan, for he had decided, as I have said, only to hold the Prussian left, to strike hardest at their right, and, when his reinforcement should come from Ney, to turn that right, envelop it, and so destroy the whole Prussian army.

These villages upon the Prussian right were taken and retaken in a series of furious attacks and counter-attacks, which it would be as tedious to detail as it must have been intolerable to endure.

All this indecisive but furious struggle for the line of villages (not one of which was as yet carried and held permanently by the French) lasted over two hours. It was well after five o'clock when there appeared, far off, under the westering sun, a new and large body of troops advancing eastward as though to reach that point between Wagnelée and St Amand where the left of the French force was struggling for mastery with the right of the Prussians. For a moment there was no certitude as to what this distant advancing force might be. But soon, and just when fortune appeared for a moment to be favouring Blucher's superior numbers and the French line was losing ground, the Emperor learned that it was his First Army Corps, under the command of Erlon which was thus approaching.

At that moment—in the neighbourhood of six o'clock in the evening—Napoleon must have believed that his new and rapidly formed plan of that afternoon, with its urgent notes to Quatre Bras and its appeal for reinforcement, had borne fruit; a portion at least of Ney's command had been detached, as it seemed, to deliver that final and unexpected attack upon the Prussian flank which was the keystone of the whole scheme.

Coincidently with the news that those distant advancing thousands were his own men and would turn this doubtful struggle into a decisive victory for the Emperor came the news—unexplained, inexplicable—that Erlon's troops would advance no further! That huge distant body of men, isolated in the empty fields to the westward; that reinforcement upon which the fate of Napoleon and of the French army hung, drew no nearer. Watched from such a distance, they might seem for a short time to be only halted. Soon it was apparent that they were actually retiring. They passed back again, retracing their steps beyond the western horizon, and were lost to the great struggle against the Prussians. Why this amazing countermarch, with all its catastrophic consequences was made will be discussed later. It is sufficient to note that it rendered impossible that decisive victory which Napoleon had held for a moment within his grasp. His resource under such a disappointment singularly illustrates the nature of his mind.

Already the Emperor had determined, before any sign of advancing aid had appeared, that if he were left alone to complete the decision, if he was not to be allowed by fate to surround and destroy the Prussian force, he might at least drive it from the field with heavy loss, and, as far as possible, demoralised. In the long struggle of the afternoon he had meant but to press the Prussian line, while awaiting forces that should complete its envelopment; these forces being now denied him, he determined to change his plan, to use his reserves, the Guard, and to drive the best fighting material he had, like a spearhead, at the centre of the Prussian positions. Since he could not capture, he would try and break.

As the hope of aid from Erlon's First Corps gradually disappeared, he decided upon this course. It was insufficient. He could not hope by it to destroy his enemy wholly. But he could drive him from the field and perhaps demoralise him, or so weaken him with loss as to leave him crippled.

Just at the time when Napoleon had determined thus to strike at the centre of the Prussian fine, Blucher, full of his recent successes upon his right and the partial recapture of the village of St Amand, had withdrawn troops from that centre to pursue his advantage. It was the wrong moment. While Blucher was thus off with the bulk of his men towards St Amand, the Old Guard, with the heavy cavalry of the Guard, and Milhaud's cavalry as well—all Napoleon's reserve—drew up opposite Ligny village for a final assault.

Nearly all the guns of the Guard and all those of the Fourth Corps crashed against the village to prepare the assault, and at this crisis of the battle, as though to emphasise its character, a heavy thunderstorm broke over the combatants, and at that late hour (it was near seven) darkened the evening sky.

It was to the noise and downpour of that storm that the assault was delivered, the Prussian centre forced, and Ligny taken.

When the clouds cleared, a little before sunset, this strongest veteran corps of Napoleon's army had done the business. Ligny was carried and held. The Prussian formation, from a convex line, was now a line bent inwards at its centre and all but broken.

Blucher had rapidly returned from the right to meet the peril. He charged at the head of his Uhlans. The head of the French column of Guards reserved their fire until the horse was almost upon them; then, in volley after volley at a stone's-throw range, they broke that cavalry, which, in their turn, the French cuirassiers charged as it fled and destroyed it. Blucher's own horse was shot under him, the colonel of the Uhlans captured, the whole of the Prussian centre fell into disorder and was crushed confusedly back towards the Nivelles-Namur road.

Darkness fell, and nothing more could be accomplished. The field was won, indeed, but the Prussian army was still an organisation and a power. It had lost heavily in surrenders, flight, and fallen, but its main part was still organised. It was driven to retreat in the darkness, but remained ready, when time should serve, to reappear. It kept its order against the end of the French pressure throughout the last glimmer of twilight; and when darkness fell, the troops of Blucher, though in retreat, were in a retreat compact and orderly, and the bulk of his command was saved from the enemy and available for further action.

Thus ended the battle of Ligny, glorious for the Emperor, who had achieved so much success against great odds and after the hottest combat; but a failure of his full plan, for the host before him was still in existence: it was free to retreat in what direction, east or north, it might choose. The choice was made with immediate and conquering decision: the order passed in the darkness, "By Tilly on Wavre." The Prussian staff had not lost its head under the blow of its defeat. It preserved a clear view of the campaign, with its remaining chances, and the then beaten army corps were concentrated upon a movement northwards. Word was sent to the fresh and unused Fourth Corps to join the other three at *Wavre*, and the march was begun which permitted Blucher, forty hours later, to come up on the flank of the French at Waterloo and destroy them.

QUATRE BRAS

Such had been the result of the long afternoon's work upon the right-hand or eastern battlefield, that of Ligny, where Napoleon had been in personal command.

In spite of his appeals, no one had reached him from the western field, and the First Corps had only appeared in Napoleon's neighbourhood to disappear again.

What had been happening on that western battlefield, three to four miles away, which had thus prevented some part at least of Ney's army coming up upon the flank of the Prussians at Ligny, towards the end of the day, and inflicting upon Blucher a complete disaster?

What had happened was the slow, confused action known to history as the battle of Quatre Bras.

It will be remembered that Ney had been entrusted by Napoleon with the absolute and independent command of something less than half of his whole army.[7]

He had put at his disposal the First and the Second Army Corps, under Erlon and Reille respectively—nearly 46,000 men; and to these he had added, by an afterthought, eight regiments of heavy cavalry, commanded by Kellerman.

---

[7] To be accurate, not quite five-twelfths.

The rôle of this force, in Napoleon's intention, was simply to advance up the Brussels road, brushing before it towards the left or west, away from the Prussians, as it went, the outposts of that western half of the allied army, which Wellington commanded.

We have seen that Napoleon, who had certainly arrived quickly and half-unexpectedly at the point of junction between Wellington's scattered forces and those of the Prussians, when he crossed the Sambre at Charleroi, overestimated his success. He thought his enemy had even less notice of his advance than that enemy really had; he thought that enemy had had less time to concentrate than he had really had. Napoleon therefore necessarily concluded that his enemy had concentrated to a less extent than he actually had.

That mistake had the effect, in the case of the army of the right, which he himself commanded, of bringing him up against not one Prussian army corps but three. This accident had not disconcerted him, for he hoped to turn it into a general disaster for the Prussians, and to take advantage of their unexpected concentration to accomplish their total ruin. But such a plan was dependent upon the left-hand or western army, that upon the Brussels road under Ney, not finding anything serious in front of it. Ney could spare men less easily if the Emperor's calculation of the resistance likely to be found on the Brussels road should be wrong. It was wrong. That resistance was not slight but considerable, and Ney was not free to come to Napoleon's aid. Tardy as had been the information conveyed to the Duke of Wellington, and grievously as the Duke of Wellington had misunderstood its importance, there was more in front of Ney upon the Brussels road than the Emperor had expected. What there was, however, might have been pushed back—after fairly heavy fighting it is true, but without any risk of failure—but for another factor in the situation, which was Ney's own misjudgment and inertia.

Napoleon himself said later that his marshal was no longer the same man since the disasters of two years before; but even if Ney had been as alert as ever, misjudgment quite as much as lack of will must have entered into what he did. He had thought, as the Emperor had, that there would be hardly anything in front of him upon the Brussels road. But there was this difference between the two errors: Ney was on the spot, and could have found out with his cavalry scouts quite early on the morning of Friday the 16th what he really had to face. He preferred to take matters for granted, and he paid a heavy price. He thought that there was plenty of time for him to advance at his leisure; and, thinking this, he must have further concluded that to linger upon that part of the Brussels road which was nearest the Emperor's forthcoming action to the east by Ligny would be good policy in case the Emperor should have need of him there.

On the night of the 15th Ney himself was at Frasnes, while the furthest of his detachments was no nearer than the bridge of Thuin over the Sambre, sixteen miles away. The rough sketch printed opposite will show how very long that line was, considering the nearness of the strategical point Quatre Bras, which it was his next business to occupy. The Second Army Corps under Reille was indeed fairly well moved up, and all in the neighbourhood of Gosselies by the night between Thursday 15th and Friday 16th of June. But the other half of the force, the First Army Corps under Erlon, was strung out over miles of road behind.

To concentrate all those 50,000 men, half of them spread out over so much space, meant a day's ordinary marching; and one would have thought that Ney should have begun to concentrate before night fell upon the 15th. He remembered, however, that the men were fatigued, he thought he had plenty of time before him, and he did not effect their concentration. The mass of the Second Army Corps (Reille's) was, as I have said, near Gosselies on the Friday dawn; but Erlon, with the First Army Corps, was not in disposition to bring the bulk of it up by the same time. He could not expect to be near Quatre Bras till noon or one o'clock. But even to this element of delay, due to his lack of precision, Ney added further delay, due to slackness in orders.

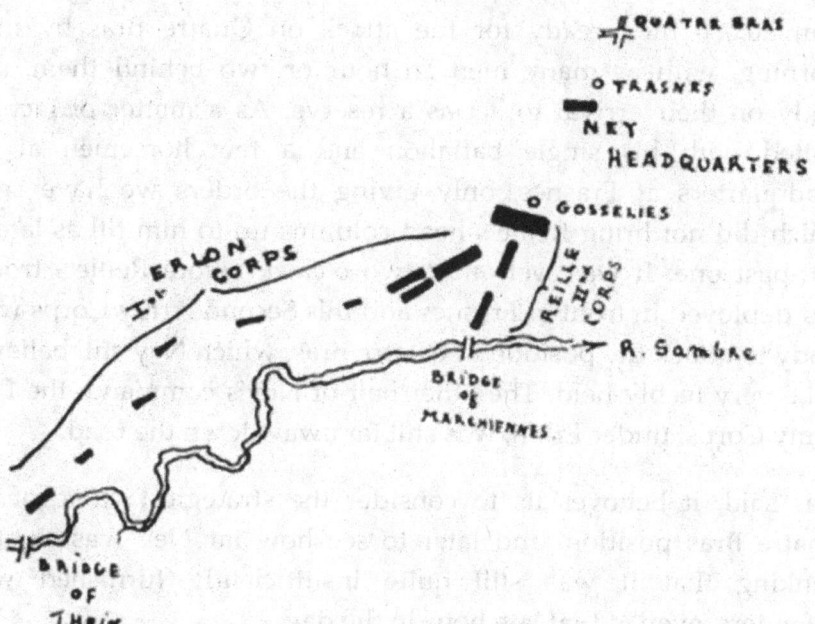

It was eleven o'clock on the morning of that Friday the 16th before Ney sent a definite order to Reille to march; it was *twelve* before the head of that Second Army Corps set out up the great road to cover the four or five miles that separated them from Ney's headquarters at Frasnes. Erlon, lying next behind Reille, could not advance until Reille's last division had taken the road. So Erlon, with the First Army Corps, was not in column and beginning his advance with his head troops until after one o'clock.

At about half-past one, then, we have the first troops of Reille's army corps reaching Ney at Frasnes, its tail-end some little way out of Gosselies; while at the same hour we have Erlon's First Army Corps marching in column through Gosselies.

It would have been perfectly possible, at the expense of a little fatigue to the men, to have had the Second Army Corps right up at Frasnes and in front of it and deployed for action by nine o'clock, while Erlon's army corps, the First, coming behind it as a reserve, an equal body in numbers, excellence, and order, would have taken the morning to come up. In other words, Ney could have had more than 20,000 men ready for the attack on Quatre Bras by midmorning, with as many men an hour or two behind them, and ready on their arrival to act as a reserve. As a matter of fact, he waited with his single battalion and a few horsemen at his headquarters at Frasnes, only giving the orders we have seen, which did not bring Reille's head columns up to him till as late as half-past one. It was well after two o'clock before Reille's troops had deployed in front of Frasnes and this Second Army Corps were ready to attack the position at Quatre Bras, which Ney still believed to be very feebly held. The other half of Ney's command, the First Army Corps, under Erlon, was still far away down the road.

This said, it behoves us to consider the strategical value of the Quatre Bras position, and later to see how far Ney was right in thinking that it was still quite insufficiently furnished with defenders, even at that late hour in the day.

Armies must march by roads. At any rate, the army marching by road has a vast advantage over one attempting an advance across country; and the better kept-up the road the greater advantage, other things being equal, has the army using it over another army debarred from its use.

Quatre Bras is the cross-way of two great roads. The first road is that main road from north to south, leading from the frontier and Charleroi to Brussels; along this road, it was Napoleon's ultimate intention to sweep, and up this road he was on that morning of the 16th sending Ney to clear the way for him. The second road is the great road east and west from Nivelles to Namur, which was in June 1815 the main line of communication along which the two halves of the Allies could effect their junction.

The invader, then, when he held Quatre Bras, could hold up troops coming against him from the north, troops coming against him from the east, or troops coming against him from the west. He could prevent, or rather delay, their junction. He would have stepped in between.

But Quatre Bras has advantages greater than this plain and elementary strategical advantage. In the first place, it dominates the whole countryside. A patch or knoll, 520 feet above the sea, the culminating point of the plateau, is within a few yards of the cross-roads. Standing there, a few steps to the west of the highway, you look in every direction over a rolling plain, of which you occupy the highest point for some miles around.

Now, this position of the "Quatre Bras" or "Cross Roads" can be easily defended against a foe coming from the south, as were the two corps under Ney. In 1815 its defence was easier still.

A large patch of undergrowth, cut in rotation, called the Wood of Bossu, ran along the high road from Frasnes and Charleroi, flanking that road to the west, and forming cover for troops that might wish to forbid access along it. The ground falls somewhat rapidly in front of the cross-roads to a little stream, and just where the stream crosses the road is the walled farm of Gemioncourt, which can be held as an advanced position, while in front of the fields where the Wood of Bossu once stood is the group of farm buildings called Pierrepont. Finally, that arm of the cross-roads which overlooks the slope down to Gemioncourt ran partly on an embankment which could be used for defence as a ready-made earthwork.

Now, let us see what troops were actually present that Friday morning upon the allied side to defend this position against Ney's advance, and what others were near enough in the neighbourhood to come up in defence of the position during the struggle.

There was but one division of the Allies actually on the spot. This was the Netherlands division, commanded by Perponcher; and the whole of it, including gunners and sappers (it had hardly any cavalry[8] with it), was less than 8000 strong. It was a very small

---

[8] It is worth remarking that Perponcher had been told by Wellington, when he first heard of Napoleon's approach, to remain some miles off to the west at Nivelles. Wellington laboured, right up to the battle of Waterloo, under the fantastic impression that the French, or a considerable body of them, were, for some extraordinary reason, going to leave the

number to hold the extended position which the division at once proceeded to occupy. They had to cover a front of over 3000 yards, not far short of two miles.

They did not know, indeed, what Ney was bringing up against them; Wellington himself, later on, greatly underestimated the French forces on that day. Now even if Ney had had far less men than he had, it was none the less a very risky thing to disperse the division as Perponcher did, especially with no more than fourteen guns to support him,[9] but under the circumstances it turned out to be a wise risk to have taken. Ney had hesitated already, and was in a mood to be surprised at any serious resistance. The more extended the veil that was drawn before him, the better for the Allies and their card of delay. For everything depended upon time. Ney, as will be seen, had thrown away his chance of victory by his extreme dilatoriness, and during the day the Allies were to bring up unit after unit, until by nightfall nearly 40,000 men not only held Quatre Bras successfully, but pushed the French back from their attack upon it.

Perponcher, then, put a battalion and five guns in front of Gemioncourt, another battalion inside the walls of the farm, four battalions and a mounted battery before the Wood of Bossu and the farm of Pierrepont. Most of his battalions were thus stretched in front of the position of Quatre Bras, the actual Cross Roads where he left only two as a reserve.

Against the Dutchmen, thus extended, the French order to advance was given, and somewhere between half-past two and a quarter to three the French attack began. It was delivered upon Gemioncourt and the fields to the right or east of the Brussels road.

Brussels road, go round westward and attack his right. He was, as might be expected of a defensive genius, nervous for his communications. Luckily for Wellington, Perponcher simply disobeyed these orders, left Nivelles before dawn, was at Quatre Bras before sunrise, and proceeded to act as we shall see above.

[9] Or at the most sixteen.

The action that followed is one simple enough to understand by description, but difficult to express upon a map. It is difficult to express upon a map because it consisted in the repeated attack of one fixed number of men against an increasing number of men.

Ney was hammering all that afternoon with a French force which soon reached its maximum. The position against which he was hammering, though held at first by a force greatly inferior to his own, began immediately afterwards to receive reinforcement after reinforcement, until at the close of the action the defenders were vastly superior in numbers to the attackers.

I have attempted in the rough pen sketch opposite this page to express this state of affairs on the allied side during the battle by marking in successive degrees of shading the bodies of the defence in the order in which they came up, but the reader must remember the factor of time, and how all day long Wellington's command at Quatre Bras kept on swelling and swelling by driblets, as the units marched in at a hurried summons from various points behind the battlefield. This gradual reinforcement of the defence gives all its character to the action.

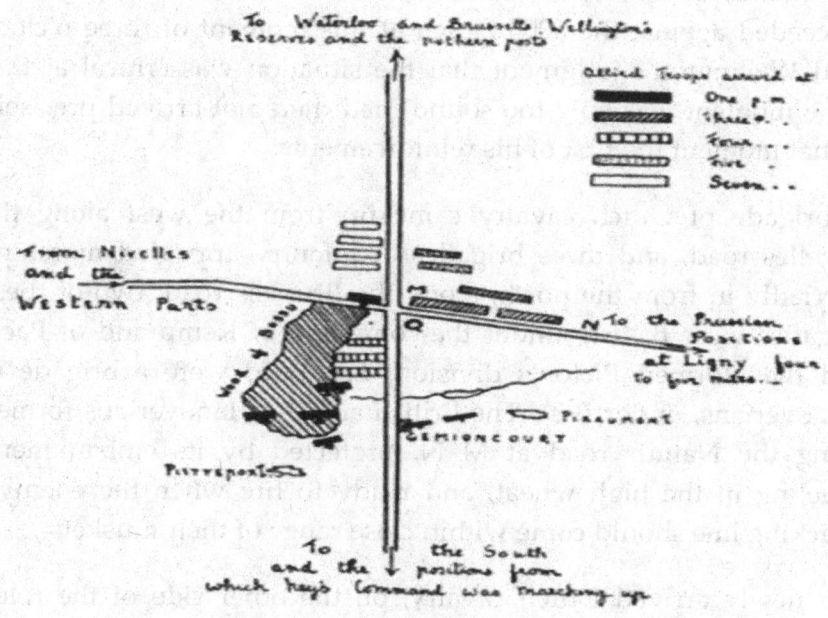

The French, then, began the assault by an advance to the right or east of the Brussels road. They cleared out the defenders from Gemioncourt; they occupied that walled position; they poured across the stream, and were beginning to take the rise up to Quatre Bras when, at about three o'clock, Wellington, who had been over at Ligny discussing the position with Blucher, rode up and saw how critical the moment was.

In a few minutes the first French division might be up to the crossroads at Q.

Bossu Wood, with the four battalions holding it, had not yet been attacked by the French, because their second division of Reille's Second Corps (under Napoleon's brother Jerome), had not yet come up; Erlon's First Corps was still far off, down the road. The men in the Bossu Wood came out to try and stop the French advance. They were thrown back by French cavalry, and even as this was proceeding Jerome's division arrived, attacked the south of Bossu Wood, and brought up the whole of Ney's forces to some 19,000 or 20,000 men.

The French advance, so continued, would now undoubtedly have succeeded against the 8000 Dutch at this moment of three o'clock (and Wellington's judgment that the situation was critical at that same moment was only too sound) had there not arrived precisely at that moment the first of his reinforcements.

A brigade of Dutch cavalry came up from the west along the Nivelles road, and three brigades of infantry appeared marching hurriedly in from the north, along the Brussels road; two of these brigades were British, under the command of Kemp and of Pack, and they formed Picton's division. The third were a brigade of Hanoverians, under Best. The British and the Hanoverians formed along the Namur road at M N, protected by its embankment, kneeling in the high wheat, and ready to fire when the enemy's attacking line should come within close range of their muskets.

The newly arrived Dutch cavalry, on the other side of the road, charged the advancing French, but were charged themselves in turn by French cavalry, overthrown, and in their stampede carried Wellington and his staff in a surge past the cross-roads; but the French cavalry, in its turn, was compelled to retire by the infantry fire it met when it had ridden too far. Immediately afterwards the French infantry as they reached the Namur road came unexpectedly upon the just-arrived British and Hanoverians, and were driven back in disorder by heavy volleying at close range from the embankment and the deep cover beyond.

The cavalry charge and countercharge (Jerome beginning to clear the south of the Bossu Wood), the check received by the French on the right from Picton's brigade and the Hanoverians occupied nearly an hour. It was not far short of four o'clock when Ney received that first urgent dispatch from Napoleon which told him to despatch the enemy's resistance at Quatre Bras, and then to come over eastward to Ligny and help against the Prussians.

Ney could not obey. He had wasted the whole of a precious morning, and by now, close on four o'clock in the afternoon, yet another unit came up to increase the power of the defence, and to make his chance of carrying the Quatre Bras cross-roads, of pushing back Wellington's command, of finding himself free to send men to Napoleon increasingly doubtful.

The new unit which had come up was the corps under the Duke of Brunswick, and when this arrived Wellington had for the first time a superiority of numbers over Ney's single corps (there was still no sign of Erlon) though he was still slightly inferior in guns.

However, the French advance was vigorously conducted. Nearly the whole of the Wood of Bossu was cleared. The Brunswickers, who had been sent forward along the road between Quatre Bras and Gemioncourt, were pushed back as to their infantry; their cavalry broke itself against a French battalion.

It was in this doubly unsuccessful effort that the Duke of

Brunswick, son of the famous General of the earlier Revolutionary wars, fell, shot in the stomach. He died that night in the village.

The check to this general advance of the French all along the line was again given by the English troops along the Namur road. Picton seized the moment, ordered a bayonet charge, and drove the French right down the valley. His men were in turn driven back by the time they had cleared the slope, but the check was given and the French never recovered it. Two fierce cavalry charges by the French failed to break the English line, though the Highlanders upon Pack's extreme right, close against Quatre Bras itself, were caught before they could form square, and the second phase of the battle ended in a draw.

Ney had missed the opportunity when the enemy in front of him were in numbers less than half his own; he had failed to pierce their line when reinforcements had brought up their numbers to a superiority over his own. He must now set about a far more serious business, for there was every prospect, as the afternoon advanced, that Wellington would be still further reinforced, while Ney had nothing but his original 20,000—half his command; of Erlon's coming there was not a sign! Yet another hour had been consumed in the general French advance and its repulse, which I have just described. It was five o'clock.

I beg the reader to concentrate his attention upon this point of the action—the few minutes before and after the hour of five. A number of critical things occurred in that short space of time, all of which must be kept in mind.

The first was this: A couple of brigades came in at that moment to reinforce Wellington. They gave him a 25 per cent. superiority in men, and an appreciable superiority in guns as well.

In the second place, Ney was keeping the action at a standstill, waiting until his own forces should be doubled by the arrival of Erlon's force. Ney had been fighting all this while, as I have said, with only half his command—the Second Army Corps of Reille. Erlon's First Army Corps formed the second half, and when it came up—as Ney confidently expected it to do immediately—it would double his numbers, and raise them from 20,000 to 40,000 men. With this superiority he could be sure of success, even if, as was probable, further reinforcements should reach the enemy's line. It is to be noted that it was due to Ney's own tardiness in giving orders that Erlon was coming up so late, but by now, five o'clock, the head of his columns might at any moment be seen debouching from Frasnes.

In the third place, while Ney was thus anxiously waiting for Erlon, and seeing the forces in front of him swelling to be more and more superior to his own, there came yet another message from Napoleon telling Ney how matters stood in the great action that was proceeding five miles away, urging him again with the utmost energy to have done at Quatre Bras, to come back over eastward upon the flank of the Prussians at Ligny, and so to destroy their army utterly and "to save France."

To have done with the action of Quatre Bras! But there were already superior forces before Ney! And they were increasing! If he dreamt of turning, it would be annihilation for his troops, or at the least the catching of his army's and Napoleon's between two fires. He *might* just manage when Erlon came up—and surely Erlon must appear from one moment to another—he *might* just manage to overthrow the enemy in front of him so rapidly as to have time to turn and appear at Ligny before darkness should fall, from three to four hours later.

It all hung on Erlon:—He *might*! and at that precise moment, with his impatience strained to breaking-point, and all his expectation turned on Frasnes, whence the head of Erlon's column should appear, there rode up to Ney a general officer, Delcambre by name. He came with a message. It was from Erlon.... Erlon had abandoned the road to Quatre Bras; had understood that he was not to join Ney after all, but to go east and help Napoleon! He had turned off eastward to the right two and a half miles back, and was by this time far off in the direction which would lead him to take part in the battle of Ligny!

Under the staggering blow of this news Ney broke into a fury. It meant possibly the annihilation of his body, certainly its defeat. He did two things, both unwise from the point of view of his own battle, and one fatal from the point of view of the whole campaign.

First, he launched his reserve cavalry, grossly insufficient in numbers for such a mad attempt, right at the English line, in a despairing effort to pierce such superior numbers by one desperate charge. Secondly, he sent Delcambre back—not calculating distance or time—with peremptory orders to Erlon, as his subordinate, to come back at once to the battlefield of Quatre Bras.

There was, as commander to lead that cavalry charge, Kellerman. He had but one brigade of cuirassiers: two regiments of horse against 25,000 men! It was an amazing ride, but it could accomplish nothing of purport. It thundered down the slope, breaking through the advancing English troops (confused by a mistaken order, and not yet formed in square), cut to pieces the gunners of a battery, broke a regiment of Brunswickers near the top of the hill, and reached at last the cross-roads of Quatre Bras. Five hundred men still sat their horses as the summit of the slope was reached. The brigade had cut a lane right through the mass of the defence; it had not pierced it altogether.

Some have imagined that if at that moment the cavalry of the Guard, which was still in reserve, had followed this first charge by a second, Ney might have effected his object and broken Wellington's line. It is extremely doubtful, the numbers were so wholly out of proportion to such a task. At any rate, the order for the second charge, when it came, came somewhat late. The five hundred as they reined up on the summit of the hill were met and broken by a furious cross-fire from the Namur road upon the right, from the head of Bossu Wood upon the left, while yet another unit, come up in this long succession to reinforce the defence—a battery of the King's German Legion—opened upon them with grape. The poor remnant of Kellerman's Horse turned and galloped back in confusion.

The second cavalry charge attempted by the French reserve, coming just too late, necessarily failed, and at the same moment yet another reinforcement—the first British division of the Guards, and a body of Nassauers, with a number of guns—came up to increase the now overwhelming superiority of Wellington's line.[10]

There was even an attempt at advance upon the part of Wellington.

As the evening turned to sunset, and the sunset to night, that advance was made very slowly and with increasing difficulty—and all the while Ney's embarrassed force, now confronted by something like double its own numbers, and contesting the ground yard by yard as it yielded, received no word of Erlon.

The clearing of the Wood of Bossu by the right wing of Wellington's army, reinforced by the newly arrived Guards, took more than an hour. It took as long to push the French centre back to Gemioncourt, and all through the last of the sunlight the walls of the farm were desperately held. On the left, Pierrepont was similarly held for close upon an hour. The sun had already set when the Guards debouched from the Wood of Bossu, only to be met and checked by a violent artillery fire from Pierrepont, while at the same time the remnant of the cuirassiers charged again, and broke a Belgian battalion at the edge of the wood.

By nine o'clock it was dark and the action ceased. Just as it ceased, and while, in the last glimmerings of the light, the major objects of the landscape, groups of wood and distant villages, could still be faintly distinguished against the background of the gloom, one such object seemed slowly to approach and move. It was first guessed and then perceived to be a body of men: the head of a column began to debouch from Frasnes. It was Erlon and his 20,000 returned an hour too late.

All that critical day had passed with the First Corps out of action. It

---

[10] This first division of the Guards consisted of the two brigades of Maitland and of Byng.

had *neither* come up to Napoleon to wipe out the Prussians at Ligny, *nor* come back in its countermarch in time to save Ney and drive back Wellington at Quatre Bras. It might as well not have existed so far as the fortunes of the French were concerned, and its absence from either field upon that day made defeat certain in the future, as the rest of these pages will show.

Two things impress themselves upon us as we consider the total result of that critical day, the 16th of June, which saw Ney fail to hold the Brussels road at Quatre Bras, and there to push away from the advance on Brussels Wellington's opposing force, and which also saw the successful escape of the Prussians from Ligny, an escape which was to permit them to join Wellington forty-eight hours later and to decide Waterloo.

The first is the capital importance, disastrous to the French fortunes, of Erlon's having been kept out of both fights by his useless march and countermarch.

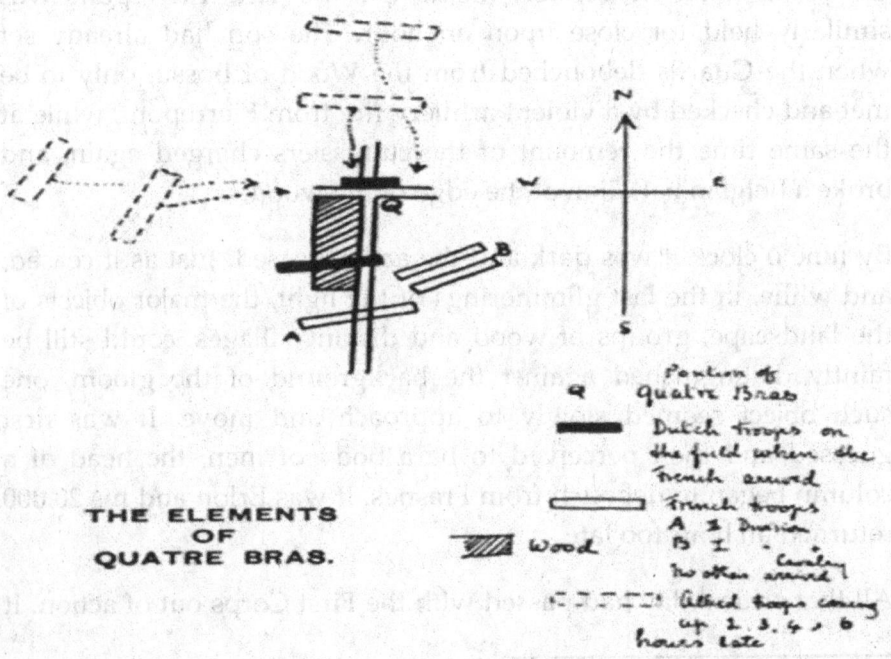

The Elements of Quatre Bras

The second is the extraordinary way in which Wellington's command came up haphazard, dribbling in by units all day long, and how that command owed to Ney's caution and tardiness, much more than to its own General's arrangements, the superiority in numbers which it began to enjoy from an early phase in the battle.

I will deal with these two points in their order.

As to the first:—

The whole of the four days of 1815, and the issue of Waterloo itself, turned upon Erlon's disastrous counter-marching between Quatre Bras and Ligny upon this Friday, the 16th of June, which was the decisive day of the war.

What actually *happened* has been sufficiently described. The useless advance of Erlon's corps d'armée towards Napoleon and the right—useless because it was not completed; the useless turning back of that corps d'armée towards Ney and the left—useless because it could not reach Ney in time,—these were the determining factors of that critical moment in the campaign.

In other words, Erlon's zigzag kept the 20,000 of the First Corps out of action all day. Had they been with Ney, the Allies under Wellington at Quatre Bras would have suffered a disaster. Had they been with Napoleon, the Prussians at Ligny would have been destroyed. As it was, the First Army Corps managed to appear on *neither* field. Wellington more than held his own; the Prussians at Ligny escaped, to fight two days later at Waterloo.

Such are the facts, and they explain all that followed (see Map, next page).

But it has rightly proved of considerable interest to historians to attempt to discover the human motives and the personal accidents of temperament and misunderstanding which led to so extraordinary a blunder as the utter waste of a whole army corps during a whole day, within an area not five miles by four.

It is for the purpose of considering these human motives and personal accidents that I offer these pages; for if we can comprehend Erlon's error, we shall fill the only remaining historical gap in the story of Waterloo, and determine the true causes of that action's result.

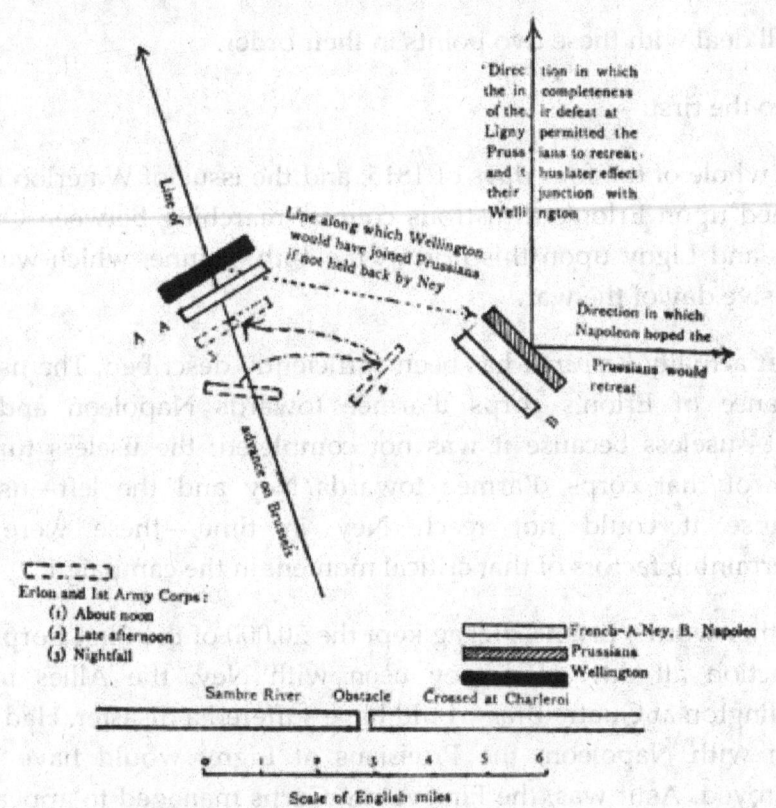

There are two ways of appreciating historical evidence. The first is the lawyer's way: to establish the pieces of evidence as a series of disconnected units, to docket them, and then to see that they are mechanically pieced together; admitting, the while, only such evidence as would pass the strict and fossil rules of our particular procedure in the courts. This way, as might be inferred from its forensic origin, is particularly adapted to arriving at a foregone conclusion. It is useless or worse in an attempt to establish a doubtful truth.

The second way is that by which we continually judge all real evidence upon matters that are of importance to us in our ordinary lives: the way in which we invest money, defend our reputation, and judge of personal risk or personal advantage in every grave case.

This fashion consists in admitting every kind of evidence, first hand, second hand, third hand, documentary, verbal, traditional, and judging the general effect of the whole, not according to set legal categories, but according to our general experience of life, and in particular of human psychology. We chiefly depend upon the way in which we know that men conduct themselves under the influence of such and such emotions, of the kind of truth and untruth which we know they will tell; and to this we add a consideration of physical circumstance, of the laws of nature, and hence of the degrees of probability attaching to the events which all this mass of evidence relates.

It is only by this second method, which is the method of commonsense, that anything can be made of a doubtful historical point. The legal method would make of history what it makes of justice. Which God forbid!

Historical points are doubtful precisely because there is conflict of evidence; and conflict of evidence is only properly resolved by a consideration of the psychology of witnesses, coupled with a consideration of the physical circumstances which limited the matter of their testimony.

Judged by these standards, the fatal march and countermarch of Erlon become plain enough.

His failure to help either Ney or Napoleon was not treason, simply because the man was not a traitor. It proceeded solely from obedience to orders; but these orders were fatal because Ney made an error of judgment both as to the real state of the double struggle—Quatre Bras, Ligny—and as to the time required for the countermarch. This I shall now show.

Briefly, then:—

Erlon, as he was leading his army corps up to help Ney, his immediate superior, turned it off the road before he reached Ney and led it away towards Napoleon.

Why did he do this?

It was because he had received, not indeed from his immediate superior, Ney himself, *but through a command of Napoleon's, which he knew to be addressed to Ney*, the order to do so.

When Erlon had almost reached Napoleon he turned his army corps right about face and led it off back again towards Ney.

Why did he do that?

It was because he had received at that moment *a further peremptory order from Ney, his direct superior, to act in this fashion*.

Such is the simple and common-sense explanation of the motives under which this fatal move and countermove, with its futile going and coming, with its apparent indecision, with its real strictness of military discipline, was conducted. As far as Erlon is concerned, it was no more than the continual obedience of orders, or supposed orders, to which a soldier is bound. With Ney's responsibility I shall deal in a moment.

Let me first make the matter plainer, if I can, by an illustration.

Fire breaks out in a rick near a farmer's house and at the same time in a barn half a mile away. The farmer sends ten men with water-buckets and an engine to put out the fire at the barn, while he himself, with another ten men, but without an engine, attends to the rick. He gives to his foreman, who is looking after the barn fire, the task of giving orders to the engine, and the man at the engine is told to look to the foreman and no one else for his orders. The foreman is known to be of the greatest authority with his master. Hardly has the farmer given all these instructions when he finds that the fire in the rick has spread to his house. He lets the barn go hang, and sends a messenger to the foreman with an urgent note to send back the engine at once to the house and rick. The messenger finds the man with the engine on his way to the barn, intercepts him, and tells him that the farmer has sent orders to the foreman that the engine is to go back at once to the house. The fellow turns round with his engine and is making his way towards the house when another messenger comes posthaste *from the foreman direct*, telling him at all costs to bring the engine back to the barn. The man with the engine turns once more, abandons the house, but cannot reach the barn in time to save it. The result of the shilly-shally is that the barn is burnt down, and the fire at the farmer's house only put out after it has done grave damage.

The farmer is Napoleon. His rick and house are Ligny. The foreman is Ney, and the barn is Quatre Bras. The man with the engine is Erlon, and the engine is Erlon's command—the First Corps d'Armée.

There was no question of *contradictory* orders in Erlon's mind, as many historians seem to imagine; there was simply, from Erlon's standpoint, a *countermanded* order.

He had received, indeed, an order coming from the Emperor, but he had received it only as the subordinate of Ney, and only, as he presumed, with Ney's knowledge and consent, either given or about to be given. In the midst of executing this order, he got another order countermanding it, and proceeding directly from his direct superior. He obeyed this second order as exactly as he had obeyed the first.

Such is, undoubtedly, the explanation of the thing, and Ney's is the mind, the person, historically responsible for the whole business.

Let us consider the difficulties in the way of accepting this conclusion. The first difficulty is that Ney would not have taken it upon himself to countermand an order of Napoleon's. Those who argue thus neither know the character of Ney nor the nature of the struggle at Quatre Bras; and they certainly underestimate both the confusion and the elasticity of warfare. Ney, a man of violent temperament (as, indeed, one might expect with such courage), was in the heat of the desperate struggle at Quatre Bras when he received Napoleon's order to abandon his own business (a course which was, so late in the action, physically impossible). Almost at the same moment Ney heard most tardily from a messenger whom Erlon had sent (a Colonel Delcambre) that Erlon, with his 20,000 men—Erlon, who had distinctly been placed under his orders—was gone off at a tangent, and was leaving him with a grossly insufficient force to meet the rapidly swelling numbers of Wellington. We have ample evidence of the rage into which he flew, and of the fact that he sent back Delcambre with the absolutely positive order to Erlon that he should turn round and come back to Quatre Bras.

Of course, if war were clockwork, if there were no human character in a commander, if no latitude of judgment were understood in the very nature of a great independent command such as Ney's was upon that day, if there were always present before every independent commander's mental vision an exact map of the operations, and, *at the same time*, a plan of the exact position of all the troops upon it at any given moment—if all these armchair conceptions of war were true, then Ney's order would have been as undisciplined in character and as foolish in intention as it was disastrous in effect.

But such conceptions are not true. Great generals entrusted with separate forces, and told off to engage in a great action at a distance from the supreme command, have, by the very nature of their mission, the widest latitude of judgment left to them. They are perfectly free to decide, in some desperate circumstance, that if their superior knew of that circumstance, he would understand why an afterorder of his was not obeyed, or was even directly countermanded. That Ney should have sent this furious counterorder, therefore, to Erlon, telling him to come back instantly, in spite of Napoleon's first note, though it was a grievous error, is one perfectly explicable, and parallel to many other similar incidents that diversify the history of war. In effect, Ney said to himself: "The Emperor has no idea of the grave crisis at *my* end of the struggle or he wouldn't have sent that order. He is winning, anyhow; I am actually in danger of defeat; and if I am defeated, Wellington's troops will pour through and come up on the Emperor's army from the rear and destroy it. I have a right, therefore, to summon Erlon back." Such was the rationale of Ney's decision. His passionate mood did the rest.

A second and graver difficulty is this: By the time Erlon got the message to come back, it was so late that he could not possibly bring his 20,000 up in time to be of any use to Ney at Quatre Bras. They could only arrive on the field, as they did in fact arrive, when darkness had already set in. It is argued that a general in Ney's position would have rapidly calculated the distance involved, and would have seen that it was useless to send for his subordinate at such an hour.

The answer to this suggestion is twofold. In the first place, a man under hot fire is capable of making mistakes; and Ney was, at the moment when he gave that order, under the hottest fire of the whole action. In the second place, he could not have any very exact idea of where in all those four miles of open fields behind him the head of Erlon's column might be, still less where exactly Delcambre would find it by the time he had ridden back. A mile either way would have made all the difference; if Erlon was anywhere fairly close; if Delcambre knew exactly where to find him, and galloped by the shortest route—if this and if that, it might still be that Erlon would turn up just before darkness and decide the field in Ney's favour.[11]

Considerable discussion has turned on whether, as the best

---

[11] Let it be remembered, for instance, that Ziethen's corps, which helped to turn the scale at Waterloo, two days later, only arrived, on the field of battle less than half an hour before sunset.

authorities believe, Erlon did or did not receive a pencilled note written personally to him by the Emperor, telling him to turn at once and come to his, Napoleon's, aid, and by his unexpected advent upon its flank destroy the Prussian army.

As an explanation of the false move of Erlon back and forth, the existence of this note is immaterial. The weight of evidence is in its favour, and men will believe or disbelieve it according to the way in which they judge human character and motive. For the purposes of a dramatic story the incident of a little pencilled note to Erlon is very valuable, but as an elucidation of the historical problem it has no importance, for, even if he got such a note, Erlon only got it in connection with general orders, which, he knew, were on their way to *Ney*, his superior.

The point for military history is that—

(*a*) Erlon, with the First Corps, on his way up to Quatre Bras that afternoon, was intercepted by a messenger, who told him that the Emperor wanted him to turn off eastward and go to Ligny, and not to Quatre Bras; while—

(*b*) He also knew that that message was intended also to be delivered, and either had been or was about to be delivered, to his superior officer, Ney. Therefore he went eastward as he had been told, believing that Ney knew all about it; and therefore, also, on receiving a further direct order from Ney to turn back again westward, he did turn back.

If we proceed to apportion the blame for that disastrous episode, which, by permitting Blucher to escape, was the plain cause of Napoleon's subsequent defeat at Waterloo, it is obvious that the blame must fall upon Ney, who could not believe, in the heat of the violent action in which he was involved, that Napoleon's contemporary action against Ligny could be more decisive or more important than his own. It was a question of exercising judgment, and of deciding whether Napoleon had justly judged the proportion between his chances of a great victory and Ney's chances; and further, whether a great victory at Ligny would have been of more effect than a great victory or the prevention of a bad defeat at Quatre Bras. Napoleon was right and Ney was wrong.

I have heard or read the further suggestion that Napoleon, on seeing Erlon, or having him reported, not two miles away, should have sent him further peremptory orders to continue his march and to come on to Ligny.

This is bad history. Erlon, as it was, was heading a trifle too much to the south, so that Napoleon, who thought the whole of Ney's command to be somewhat further up the Brussels road northward than it was, did not guess at first what the new troops coming up might be, and even feared they might be a detachment of Wellington's, who might have defeated Ney, and now be coming in from the west to attack *him*.

He sent an orderly to find out what the newcomers were. The orderly returned to report that the troops were Erlon's, but that they had turned back. Had Napoleon sent again, after this, to find Erlon, and to make him for a third time change his direction, it would have been altogether too late to have used Erlon's corps d'armée at Ligny by the time it should have come up. Napoleon had, therefore, no course before him but to do as he did, namely, give up all hope of help from the west, and defeat the Prussians at Ligny before him, if not decisively, at least to the best of his ability, with the troops immediately to his hand.

So much for Erlon.

Now for the second point: the way in which the units of Wellington's forces dribbled in all day haphazard upon the position of Quatre Bras.

Wellington, as we saw on an earlier page, was both misinformed and confused as to the nature and rapidity of the French advance into Belgium. He did not appreciate, until too late, the importance of the position of Quatre Bras, nor the intention of the French to march along the great northern road. Even upon the field of Waterloo itself he was haunted by the odd misconception that Napoleon's army would try and get across his communications with the sea, and he left, while Waterloo was actually being fought, a considerable force useless, far off upon his right, on that same account.

The extent of Wellington's misjudgment we can easily perceive and understand. Every general must, in the nature of war, misjudge to some extent the nature of his opponent's movements, but the shocking errors into which bad staff work led him in this his last campaign are quite exceptional.

Wellington wrote to Blucher, on his arrival at the field of Quatre Bras, at about half-past ten in the morning, a note which distinctly left Blucher to understand that he might expect English aid during his forthcoming battle with Napoleon at Ligny. He did not say so in so many words, but he said: "My forces are at such and such places," equivalent, that is, to saying, "My forces can come up quite easily, for they are close by you," adding: "I do not see any large force of the enemy in front of us; and I await news from your Highness, and the arrival of troops, in order to determine my operations for the day."

In this letter, moreover, he said in so many words that his reserve, the large body upon which he mainly depended, would be within three miles of him by noon, the British cavalry within seven miles of him at the same hour.

Then he rode over to see Blucher on the field of Ligny before Napoleon's attack on that general had begun. He got there at about one o'clock.

An acrimonious discussion has arisen as to whether he promised to come up and help Blucher shortly afterwards or not, but it is a discussion beside the mark, for, in the first place, Wellington quite certainly *intended* to come up and help the Prussians; and in the second place, he was quite as certainly *unable* to do so, for the

French opposition under Ney which he had under-estimated, turned out to be a serious thing.

But his letter, and his undoubted intention to come up and help Blucher, depended upon his belief that the units of his army were all fairly close, and that by, say, half-past one he would have the whole lot occupying the heights of Quatre Bras.

Now, as a fact, the units of Wellington's command were scattered all over the place, and it is astonishing to note the discrepancy between his idea of their position and their real position on the morning of the day when Quatre Bras was fought. When one appreciates what that discrepancy was, one has a measure of the bad staff work that was being done under Wellington at the moment.

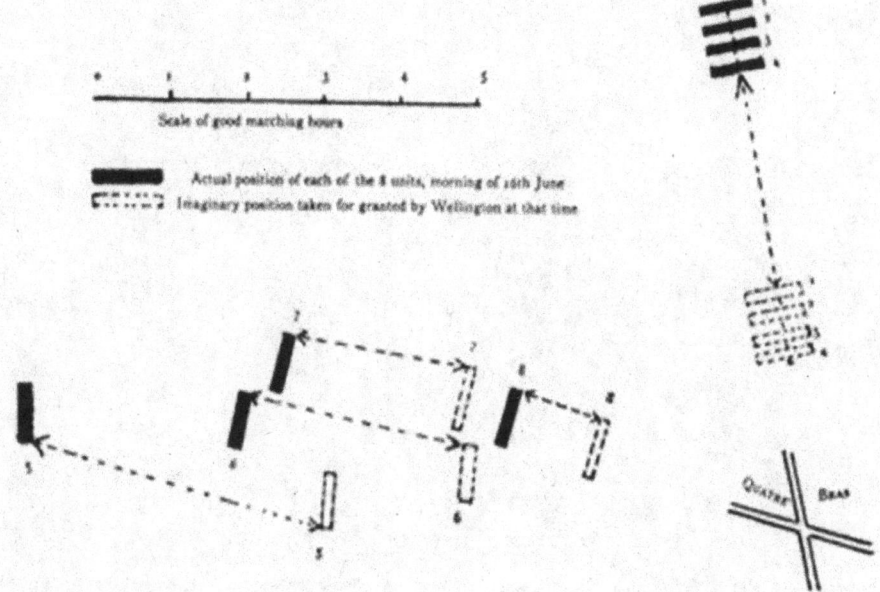

The plan (p. 127)[12] distinguishes between the real positions of

---

[12] I have in this map numbered separate corps and units from one to ten, without giving them names. The units include the English cavalry and Dornberg's brigade, with the Cumberland Hussars, the First, Second, Third, and Fifth Infantry Divisions, the corps of Brunswick, the Nassauers,

Wellington's command on the morning of the 16th when he was writing his letter to Blucher and the positions which Wellington, in that letter, erroneously ascribes to them. It will show the reader the wide difference there was between Wellington's idea of where his troops were and their actual position on that morning. It needs no comment. It is sufficient in itself to explain why the action at Quatre Bras consisted not in a set army meeting and repelling the French (it could have destroyed them as things turned out, seeing Erlon's absence), but in the perpetual arrival of separate and hurried units, which went on from midday almost until nightfall.

---

and the Second and Third Netherlands Divisions. All of these ultimately reached Quatre Bras with the exception of the Second Infantry Division.

IV

THE ALLIED RETREAT AND FRENCH ADVANCE UPON WATERLOO AND WAVRE

When the Prussians had concentrated to meet Napoleon at Ligny they had managed to collect, in time for the battle, three out of their four army corps.

These three army corps were the First, the Second, and the Third, and, as we have just seen, they were defeated.

But, as we have also seen, they were not thoroughly defeated. They were not disorganised, still less were the bulk of them captured and disarmed. Most important of all, they were free to retreat by any road that did not bring them against their victorious enemy. In other words, they were free to retreat to the north as well as to the east.

The full importance of this choice will, after the constant reiteration of it in the preceding pages, be clear to the reader. A retreat towards the east, and upon the line of communications which fed the Prussian army, would have had these two effects: First, it would have involved in the retirement that fresh Fourth Army Corps under Bulow which had not yet come into action, and which numbered no less than 32,000 men. For it lay to the east of the battlefield. In other words, that army corps would have been wasted, and the whole of the Prussian forces would have been forced out of the remainder of the campaign. Secondly, it would have finally separated Blucher and his Prussians from Wellington's command. The Duke, with his western half of the allied forces, would have had to stand up alone to the mass of Napoleon's army, which would, after the defeat of the Prussians at Ligny, naturally turn to the task of defeating the English General.

Now the fact of capital importance upon which the reader must concentrate if he is to grasp the issue of the campaign is the fact that the French staff fell into an error as to the true direction of the Prussian retreat.

Napoleon, Soult, and all the heads of the French army were convinced that the Prussian retreat *was* being made by that eastern road.

As a fact, the Prussians, under the cover of darkness, had retired *not* east but north.

The defeated army corps, the First, Second, and Third, did not fall back upon the fresh and unused Fourth Corps; they left it unhampered to march northward also; and all during the darkness the Prussian forces, as a whole, were marching in roughly parallel columns upon Wavre and its neighbourhood.

It was this escape to the north instead of the east that made it possible for the Prussians to effect their junction with Wellington upon the day of Waterloo; but it must not be imagined that this supremely fortunate decision to abandon the field of their defeat at Ligny in a northerly rather than an easterly direction was at first deliberately conceived by the Prussians with the particular object of effecting a junction with Wellington later on.

In the first place, the Prussians had no idea what line Wellington's retreat would take. They knew that he was particularly anxious about his communications with the sea, and quite as likely to move westward as northward when Napoleon should come against him.

The full historical truth, accurately stated, cannot be put into the formula, "The Prussians retreated northward in order to be able to join Wellington two days later at Waterloo." To state it so would be to read history backwards, and to presuppose in the Prussian staff a knowledge of the future. The true formula is rather as follows:— "The Prussians retired northward, and not eastward, because the incompleteness of their defeat permitted them to do so, and thus at once to avoid the waste of their Fourth Army Corps and to gain positions where they would be able, if necessity arose, to get news of what had happened to Wellington."

In other words, to retreat northwards, though the decision to do so depended only upon considerations of the most general kind, was wise strategy, and the opportunity for that piece of strategy was seized; but the retreat northwards was not undertaken with the specific object of at once rejoining Wellington.

It must further be pointed out that this retreat northwards, though it abandoned the fixed line of communications leading through Namur and Liège to Aix la Chapelle, would pick up in a very few miles another line of communications through Louvain, Maestricht, and Cologne. The Prussian commanders, in determining upon this northward march, were in no way risking their supply nor hazarding the existence of their army upon a great chance. They were taking advantage of one of two courses left open to them, and that one the wiser of the two.

This retreat upon Wavre was conducted with a precision and an endurance most remarkable when we consider the fact that it took place just after a severe, though not a decisive, defeat.

Of the eighty odd thousand Prussians engaged at Ligny, probably 12,000 had fallen, killed or wounded. When the Prussian centre broke, many units became totally disorganised; and, counting the prisoners and runaways who failed to rejoin the colours, we must accept as certainly not exaggerated the Prussian official report of a loss of 15,000.[13]

In spite, I say, of this severe defeat, the order of the retreat was well maintained, and was rewarded by an exceptional rapidity.

---

[13] In which 15,000, as accurate statistics are totally lacking, and the whole thing is a matter of rough estimate, we may assign what proportion we will to killed, to wounded, and to prisoners respectively.

The First Corps marched along the westerly route that lay directly before them by Tilly and Mont St Guibert. They marched past Wavre itself, and bivouacked about midday of Saturday the 17th, round about the village of Bierges, on the other side of the river Dyle.

The Second Corps followed the First, and ended its march on the southern side of Wavre, round about the village of St Anne.

The Third Corps did not complete the retreat until the end of daylight upon the 17th, and then marched through Wavre, across the river to the north, and bivouacked around La Bavette.

Finally, still later on the same evening, the Fourth Corps, that of Bulow, which had come to Ligny too late for the action, marching by the eastward lanes, through Sart and Corry, lay round Dion Le Mont.

By nightfall, therefore, on Saturday the 17th of June, we have the mass of the Prussian army safe round Wavre, and duly disposed all round that town in perfect order.

With the exception of a rearguard, which did not come up until the morning of the Sunday, all had been safely withdrawn in the twenty-four hours that followed the defeat at Ligny.

It may be asked why this great movement had been permitted to take place without molestation from the victors.

Napoleon would naturally, of course, after his defeat of the Prussians, withdraw to the west the greater part of the forces he had used against Blucher at Ligny and direct them towards the Brussels road in order to use them next against Wellington. But Napoleon had left behind him Grouchy in supreme command over a great body of troops, some 33,000 in all, whose business it was to follow up the Prussians, to find out what road they had taken; at the least to watch their movements, and at the best to cut off any isolated bodies or to give battle to any disjointed parts which the retreat might have separated from support. In general, Grouchy was to see to it that the Prussians did not return.

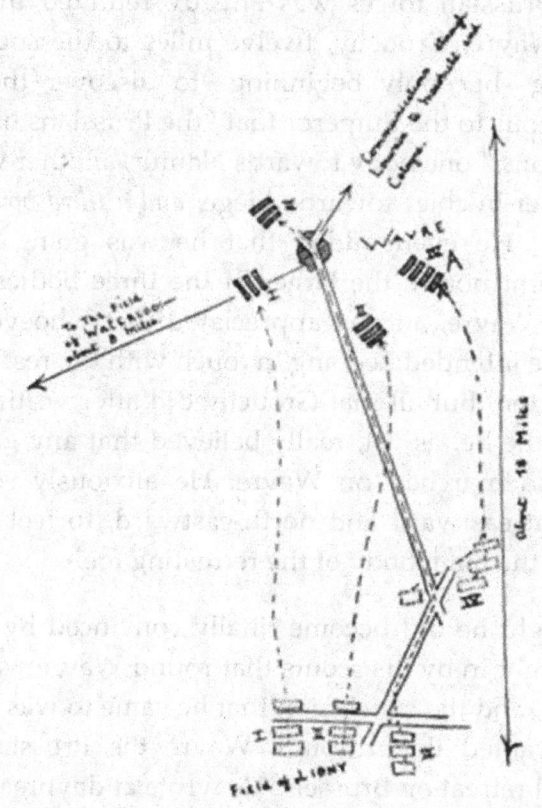

In this task Grouchy failed. True, he was not given his final instructions by the Emperor until nearly midday of the 17th, but a man up to his work would have discovered the line of the Prussian retreat and have hung on to it. Grouchy failed, partly because he was insufficiently provided with cavalry, partly because he was a man excellent only in a sudden tactical dilemma, incompetent in large strategical problems, partly because he mistrusted his subordinates, and they him; but most of all because of an original prepossession (under which, it is but fair to him to add, all the French leaders lay) that the Prussian retreat had taken the form of a flight towards Namur, along the eastern line of communications, while, as a fact, it had taken the form of a disciplined retreat upon Wavre and the north.

At ten o'clock in the evening of Saturday the 17th, twenty-four hours after the battle of Ligny, and at the moment when the whole body of the Prussian forces was already reunited in an orderly circle round Wavre, Grouchy, twelve miles to the south of them, was beginning—but only beginning—to discover the truth. He wrote at that hour to the Emperor that "the Prussians had retired in several directions," one body towards Namur, another with Blucher the Commander-in-chief towards Liège, *and a third body apparently towards Wavre*. He even added that he was going to find out whether it might not be the larger of the three bodies which had gone towards Wavre, and he appreciated that whoever had gone towards Wavre intended keeping in touch with the rest of the Allies under Wellington. But all that Grouchy did after writing this letter proves how little he, as yet, really believed that any great body of the enemy had marched on Wavre. He anxiously sent out, not northward, but eastward and north-eastward, to feel for what he believed to be the main body of the retreating foe.

During the night he did become finally convinced by the mass of evidence brought in by his scouts that round Wavre was the whole Prussian force, and the conclusion that he came to was singular! He took it for granted that through Wavre the Prussians certainly intended a full retreat on Brussels. He wrote at daybreak of the 18th of June that he was about to pursue them.

That Blucher could dream of taking a short cut westward, thus effecting an immediate junction with Wellington, never entered Grouchy's head. He did not put his army in motion until after having written this letter. He advanced his troops in a decent and leisurely manner up the Wavre road through the mid hours of the day, and himself, just before noon, wrote a dispatch to the Emperor; he wrote it from Sart, a point ten miles south of Wavre. In that letter he announced "his intention to be massed at Wavre *that night*," and begging for "orders as to how he should begin his attack of the *next day*."

The next day! Monday!

Already, hours before—by midnight of Saturday—Blucher had sent his message to Wellington assuring him that the Prussians would come to his assistance upon Sunday, the morrow.

Even as Grouchy was writing, the Prussian Corps were streaming westward across country to appear upon Napoleon's flank four hours later and decide the campaign.

Having written his letter, Grouchy sat down to lunch. As he sat there at meat, far off, the first shots of the battle of Waterloo were fired.

So far, we have followed the retreat of the Prussians northwards from their defeat at Ligny. With the exception of the rearguard, they were all disposed by the evening of Saturday the 17th in an orderly fashion round the little town of Wavre. We have also followed the methodical but tardy and ill-conceived pursuit in which Grouchy felt out with his cavalry to discover the line of the Prussian retreat, and continued to be in doubt of its nature at least until midnight, and probably until even later than midnight, in that night between Saturday the 17th, evening, and Sunday the 18th of June.

We have further seen that during the morning of Sunday the 18th of June he was taking no dispositions for a rapid pursuit, but, being now convinced that the Prussians merely intended a general retreat upon Brussels, proposed to follow them in order to watch that retreat, and, if possible, to shepherd them eastwards. He wrote, as we have just said, to the Emperor in the course of that morning of the Sunday, announcing that he meant to mass his troops at Wavre by nightfall, and asking for orders for the next day.

What the Prussians were doing during that Sunday morning when Grouchy was so quietly and soberly taking for granted that they could not or would not rejoin Wellington, and was so quietly shielding his own responsibility behind the Emperor's orders, we shall see when we come to talk of the action itself—the battle of Waterloo.

Meanwhile we must return to the second half of the great strategic move, and watch the retreat of the Duke of Wellington during that same Saturday, and the stand which he made on the ridge called "the Mont St Jean" by the nightfall of that day, in order to accept battle on the Sunday morning.

An observer watching the whole business of that Saturday from some height in the air above the valley of the Sambre, and looking northwards, would have seen on the landscape below, to his right, the Prussians streaming in great parallel columns upon Wavre from the battlefield of Ligny. He would have seen, scattered upon the roads, small groups of mounted men, here in touch with the last files of a Prussian column, there lost and wandering forward into empty spaces where no soldiers were. These were the cavalry scouts of Grouchy. South of these, and far behind the Prussian rear, separated from them by a gap of ten miles, a dense body of infantry, drawn up in heavy columns of route, was the corps commanded by Grouchy.

What would such an observer have seen upon the landscape below and before him to his left? He would have seen an interminable line of men streaming northward also, all afternoon, up the Brussels road from Quatre Bras; and behind them, treading upon their heels, another column, miles in length, pressing the pursuit. The retreating column, as it hurried off, he would see screened on its rear by a mass of cavalry, that from time to time charged and checked the pursuers, and sometimes put guns in line to hold them back. The pursuers, after each such check, would still press on. The first, the thousands in retreat, were Wellington's command retiring from Quatre Bras; the second, the pursuers, were a body some 74,000 strong formed by the junction of Ney and Napoleon, and pressing forward to bring Wellington to battle.

At Quatre Bras, Wellington had not been able, as he had hoped, to join the Prussians and save them from defeat. The French, under Ney, had held him up. He would even have suffered a reverse had Ney attacked promptly and strongly earlier in the day of Friday the 16th, but Ney had not acted promptly and strongly.

All day long reinforcements had come in one after the other, much later than the Duke intended, but in a sufficient measure to meet the tardy and too cautious development of Ney's attack. Finally, the real peril under which the Duke lay (though he did not know it)—the junction of Erlon and his forces with Ney—had not taken place until darkness fell, and Erlon's 20,000 had been wasted in the futile fashion which has been described and analysed.

The upshot, therefore, of the whole business at Quatre Bras was, that during the night between Friday and Saturday the 16th and the 17th the English and the French lay upon their positions, neither seriously incommoding the other.

During that night further reinforcements reached Wellington where his troops had bivouacked upon the positions they had held so well. Lord Uxbridge, in command of the British cavalry, and Ompteda's brigade both came up with the morning, as did also Clinton's division and Colville's division, and so did the reserve artillery.

In spite of all these reinforcements, in spite even of the great mass of horse which Uxbridge had brought up, and of the new guns, Wellington's position upon that morning of Saturday the 17th of June was, though he did not yet know it, very perilous.

He still believed that the Prussians were holding on to Ligny, and that they had kept their positions during the night, which night he had himself spent at Genappe, to the rear of the battlefield of Quatre Bras.[14]

---

[14] The reason he was thus ignorant of what had really happened to the Prussians was, that the officer who had been sent by the chief of the Prussian staff to the Duke after nightfall to inform him of the Prussian defeat had never arrived. That officer had been severely wounded on the way, and the message was not delivered.
This dispute is solved, as are many disputes, by the consideration that each narrator is right from his point of view. The French pursuit was most vigorous, the English rearguard was very hard pressed indeed; but that

When Wellington awoke on the morning of Saturday in Genappe, there were rumours in the place that the Prussians had been defeated the day before at Ligny. The Duke went at once to Quatre Bras; sent Colonel Gordon off eastward with a detachment of the Tenth Hussars to find out what had happened, and that officer, finding the road from Ligny in the hands of the French, had the sense to scout up northwards, came upon the tail of the Prussian retreat, and returned to Wellington at Quatre Bras by half-past seven with the whole story: the Prussians had indeed been beaten; they were in full retreat; but a chance of retreat had lain open towards the north, and that was the road they had taken.

Wellington knew, therefore, before eight o'clock on that Saturday morning, that his whole left or eastern flank was exposed, and it was common-sense to expect that Napoleon, with the main body of the French, having defeated the Prussians at Ligny, would now march against himself, come up upon that exposed flank (while Ney held the front), and so outnumber the Anglo-Dutch under the Duke's command. At the worst that command would be destroyed; at the best it could only hope, if it gave time for Napoleon to come up, to have to retreat westward, and to lose touch, for good, with the Prussians.

In such a plight it was Wellington's business to retreat towards the north, so as to remain in touch with his Prussian allies, while yet that line of retreat was open to him, and before Napoleon should have forced a battle.

The Duke was in no hurry to undertake this movement, for as yet there was no sign of Napoleon's arrival. The men breakfasted, and it was not until ten o'clock that the retreat began. He sent word back up the road to stop the reinforcements that were still upon their way to join him at Quatre Bras, and to turn them round again

---

rearguard was so well handled that it continually held its own, gave back as good as it got, and efficiently protected the unmolested retreat of the mass of the army.

up the Brussels road, the way they had come, until they should reach the ridge of the Mont St Jean, just in front of the village of Waterloo, where he had determined to stand. This done, he made his dispositions for retirement, and a little after ten o'clock the retreat upon Waterloo began. His English infantry led the retreat, the Netherland troops following, then the Brunswickers, and the last files of that whole great body of men were marching up the Brussels road northward before noon. Meanwhile, Lord Uxbridge, with his very considerable force of cavalry and the guns necessary to support it, deployed to cover the retreat, and watched the enemy.

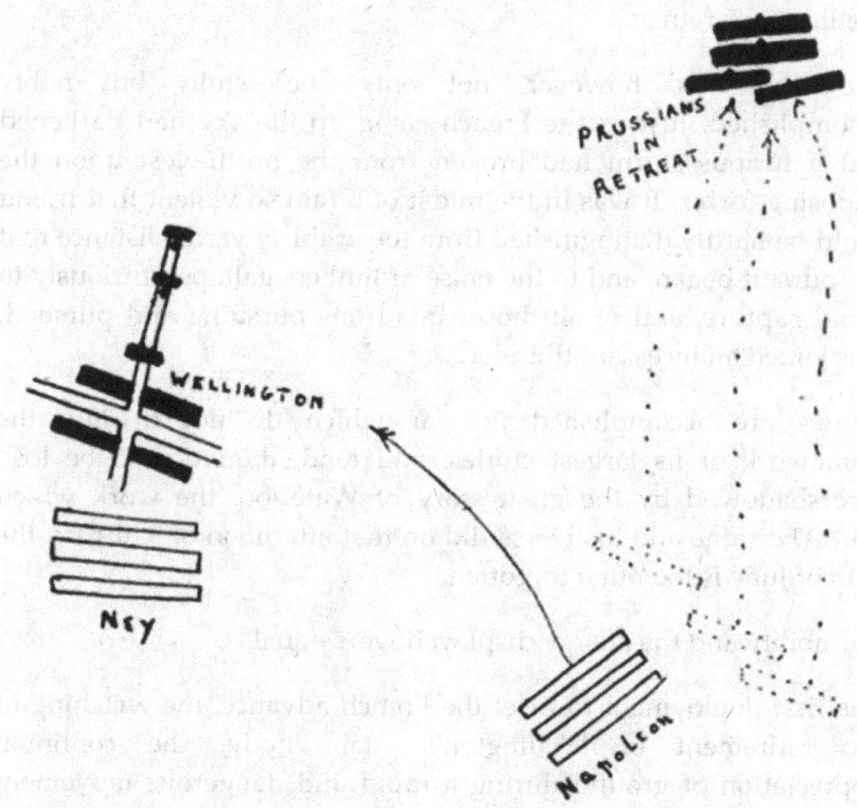

Sketch showing the situation in which Wellington was at Quatre Bras on the morning of the 17th.

That enemy was motionless. Ney did not propose to attack until Napoleon should come up. Napoleon and his troops, arriving from the battlefield of Ligny, were not visible until within the neighbourhood of two o'clock. As he came near the Emperor was perceived, his memorable form distinguished in the midst of a small escorting body, urging the march; and the English guns, during one of those rare moments in which war discovers something of drama, fired upon the man who was the incarnation of all that furious generation of arms. In a military study, this moment, valuable to civilian history, may be neglected.

The flood of French troops arriving made it hard for Uxbridge, in spite of his very numerous cavalry and supporting guns, to cover Wellington's retreat.

The task was, however, not only successfully but nobly accomplished. Just as the French came up the sky had darkened and a furious storm had broken from the north-west upon the opposing forces. It was in the midst of a rain so violent that friend could be hardly distinguished from foe at thirty yards distance that the pursuit began, and to the noise of limbers galloped furiously to avoid capture, and of all those squadrons pursuing and pursued, was joined an incessant thunder.

Things are accomplished in war which do not fit into the framework of its largest stories, and tend, therefore, to be lost. Overshadowed by the great story of Waterloo, the work which Lord Uxbridge and his Horse did on that afternoon of Saturday the 17th of June is too often forgotten.

The ability and the energy displayed were equal.

The first deployment to meet the French advance, the watching of the retirement of Wellington's main body, the continual appreciation of ground during a rapid and dangerous movement and in the worst of weather, the choice of occasional artillery positions—all these showed mastery, and secured the complete order of Wellington's retreat.[15]

---

[15] There has arisen a discussion as to the whole nature of this retreat between the French authorities, who insist upon the close pursuit by their

The pursuit was checked at its most important point (where the French had to cross the river Dyle at Genappe) by a rapid deployment of the cavalry upon the slope beyond the stream, a rapid unlimbering of the batteries in retreat, and a double charge, first of the Seventh Hussars, next of the First Life Guards.

These charges were successful, they checked the French, and during the remainder of the afternoon the pursuit to the north of the Dyle slackened off until, before darkness, it ceased altogether.

Indeed, there was by that time no further use in it. The mass of Wellington's army had reached, and had deployed upon, that ridge of the Mont St Jean where he intended to turn and give battle. They were in a position to receive any immediate attack, and the purposes of mere pursuit were at an end.

Facing that ridge of the Mont St Jean, where, at the end of the afternoon and through the evening, Wellington's troops were already taking up their positions, was another ridge, best remembered by the name of a farm upon its crest, the "Belle Alliance." This ridge formed the natural halting-place of the pursuers. From the height above Genappe to the ridge of the Belle Alliance was but 5000 yards; and if a further reason be quoted for the cessation of the pursuit and the ranging into battle array of either force, the weather will provide that reason.

The soil of all these fields is of a peculiar black and consistent sort, almost impassable after a drenching rain. The great paved high road which traverses it was occupied and encumbered by the wheeled vehicles and by the artillery. A rapid advance of infantry bodies thrown out to the right and left of the road, and so securing speed by parallel advance, was made impossible by mud, and the line grew longer and longer down the main road, forbidding rapid

---

troops and the precipitate flight of the English rearguard, and the English authorities, who point out how slight were the losses of that rearguard, and how just was Wellington's comment that the retreat, as a whole, was unmolested.

movement. From mud, that "fifth element in war" (as Napoleon himself called it), Wellington's troops—the mass of them at least— had been fairly free. They had reached their positions before the downpour. Only the cavalry of the rearguard and its batteries had felt the full force of the storm. Dry straw of the tall standing crops had been cut on the ridge of the Mont St Jean, and the men of Wellington's command bivouacked as well as might be under such weather.

With the French it was otherwise. Their belated units kept straggling in until long after nightfall. The army was drawn up only at great expense of time and floundering effort, mainly in the dark, drenched, sodden with mud, along the ridge of the Belle Alliance. It was with difficulty that the wood of the bivouac fires could be got to burn at all. They were perpetually going out; and all that darkness was passed in a misery which the private soldier must silently expect as part of his trade, and which is relieved only by those vague corporate intuitions of a common peril, and perhaps a common glory, which, down below all the physical business, form the soul of an army.

Napoleon, when he had inspected all this and assured himself that Wellington was standing ranged upon the opposite ridge, returned to sleep an hour or two at the farm called Le Caillou, a mile behind the line of bivouacs. Wellington took up his quarters in the village of Waterloo, about a mile and a half behind the bivouacs of his troops upon the Mont St Jean.

In such a disposition the two commanders and their forces waited for the day.

There must, lastly, be considered, before the description of action is entered on, the nature of the field upon which it was about to be contested. That field had been studied by Wellington the year before. He, incomparably the greatest tactical defensive commander of his time, and one of the greatest of all time, had chosen it for its capacities of defence. They were formidable. Relying upon them, and confident of the Prussians coming to his aid when the battle was joined, he rightly counted upon success.

Let us begin by noting that of no battle is it more important to seize the exact nature of the terrain, that is, of the ground over which it was fought, than of Waterloo.

To the eye the structure of the battlefield is simple, consisting essentially of two slight and rounded ridges, separated by a very shallow undulation of land.

But this general formation is complicated by certain features which can only be grasped with the aid of contours, and these contours, again, are not very easy to follow at first sight for those who have not seen the battlefield.

In the map which forms the frontispiece of this volume, and to which I will beg the reader to turn, I have indicated the undulations of land in pale green lines underlying the other features of the battle, which are in black, red, and blue. The contours are drawn at five metres (that is 16 feet 4 inches) distance; no contours are given below that of 100 metres above the sea. The valley floors below that level are shaded. Up to the 120-metre line the contours are indicated by continuous lines of increasing thickness. Above the 120-metre line they are indicated by faint dotted or dashed lines. I hope in this manner, though the task is a difficult one, to give a general impression of the field.

The whole field, both slight ridges and the intervening depression, lies upon a large swell of land many square miles in extent, while it slopes away gradually to the east on one side and the west on the other. The highest and hardly distinguishable knolls of it stand about 450 feet above the sea. The site of the battle lies actually on the highest part, the water-parting; and the floors of the valleys, down which the streams run to the east and to the west, are from 150 to 200 feet lower than this confused lift of land between. To one, however, standing upon any part of the battlefield, this feature of height is not very apparent. True, one sees lower levels falling away left and right, and the view seems oddly wide, but the eye gathers the impression of little more than a rolling plain. This is because, in comparison with the scale of the landscape as a whole, the elevations and depressions are slight.

Upon this rolling mass of high land there stand out, as I have said, those two slight ridges, and these ridges lie, roughly speaking, east and west—perpendicular to the great Brussels road, which cuts them from south to north. It was upon this great Brussels road that both Wellington and Napoleon took up, at distances less than a mile apart, their respective centres of position for the struggle. Though this line of the road did not precisely bisect the two lines of the opposing armies, the point where it crossed each line marked the tactical centre of that line: both Wellington and Napoleon remained in person upon that road.

Now it must not be imagined that the shallow depression between the ridges stretches of even depth between the two positions taken up by Wellington and Napoleon, with the road cutting its middle; on the contrary, it is bridged, a little to the west of the road, by a "saddle," a belt of fields very nearly flat, and very nearly as high as each ridge. The eastern half of the depression therefore rises continually, and gets shallower and shallower as it approaches the road from east westward, and the road only cuts off the last dip of it. Then, just west of the road there is the saddle; and as you proceed still further westward along the line midway between the French and English positions you find a second shallow valley falling away. This second valley does not precisely continue the direction of the first, but turns rather more to the north. In the first slight decline of this second valley, and a few hundred yards west of the road, lies the country-house called Hougomont, and just behind it lay the western end of Wellington's line. The whole position, therefore, if it were cut out as a model in section from a block of wood, might appear as does the accompanying plan.

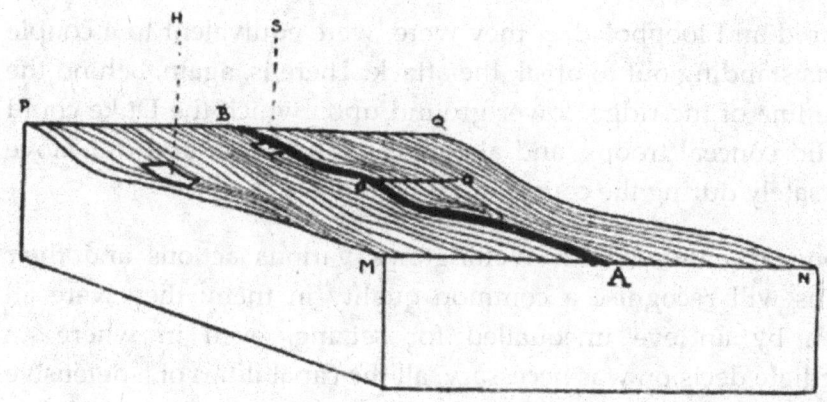

In such a model the northern ridge P—Q some two miles in length is that held by Wellington. The southern one M—N is that held by Napoleon. Napoleon commanded from the point A, Wellington from the point B, and the dark band running from one to the other represents the great Brussels High Road. The subsidiary ridge O—O is that on which Napoleon, as we shall see, planted his great battery preparatory to the assault. The enclosure H is Hougomont, the enclosure S is La Haye Sainte.

Of the two ridges, that held by Napoleon needs less careful study for the comprehension of the battle than that held by Wellington.

The latter is known as the Ridge of the Mont St Jean, from a farm lying a little below its highest point and a little behind its central axis. This ridge Wellington had carefully studied the year before, and that great master of defence had noted and admired the excellence of its defensive character. Not only does the land rise towards the ridge through the whole length of the couple of miles his troops occupied, not only is it almost free of "dead"[16] ground, but there lie before it two walled enclosures, the small one of La Haye Sainte, the large one of Hougomont, which, properly

---

[16] "Dead" ground means ground in front of a position sheltered by its very steepness from the fire of the defence upon the summit. The ideal front for a defence conducted with firearms is not a very steep slope, but a long, slight, open and even one.

prepared and loopholed as they were, were equivalent to a couple of forts standing out to break the attack. There is, again, behind the whole line of the ridge, lower ground upon which the Duke could and did conceal troops, and along which he could and did move them safely during the course of the action.

Anyone acquainted with Wellington's various actions and their terrains will recognise a common quality in them: they were all chosen by an eye unequalled for seizing, even in where an immediate decision was necessary, all the capabilities of a defensive position. That taken up on the 18th of June 1815, in the Duke's last battle, had been chosen, not under the exigencies of immediate combat, but with full leisure and after a complete study. It is little wonder, then, that it is the best example of all. Of all the defensive positions which the genius of Wellington has made famous in Europe, none excels that of Waterloo.

V

THE ACTION

In approaching this famous action, it is essential to recapitulate the strategical conditions which determined its result.

I have mentioned them at the outset and again in the middle of this study; I must repeat them here.

The only chance Napoleon had when he set forward in early June to attack the allies in Belgium, the vanguard of his enemies (who were all Europe), was a chance of surprising that vanguard, of striking in suddenly between its two halves, of thoroughly defeating one or the other, and then turning to defeat as thoroughly its colleague.

Other chances than this desperate chance he had none; for he was fighting against odds of very nearly two to one even in his attack upon this mere vanguard of the armed kings; their total forces were, of course, overwhelmingly superior.

He did succeed, as we have seen, in striking suddenly in between the two halves of the allied army in Belgium. He was not as quick as he had intended to be. There were faults and delays, but he managed, mainly through the malinformation and misjudgment of Wellington, to deal with the Prussians unsupported by Wellington's western wing.

He attacked those Prussians with the bulk of his forces; and although he was outnumbered even upon that field, he defeated the Prussians at Ligny. But the defeat was not complete. The Prussians were free to retire northward, and so ultimately to rejoin Wellington. They took that opportunity, and from the moment they had taken it Napoleon was doomed.

We have further seen that Grouchy, who had been sent after the

Prussian retreat, might, if he had seen all the possibilities of that retreat, and had seen them in time, have stepped in between the Prussians and Wellington, and have prevented the appearance of the former upon the field of Waterloo.

Had Grouchy done so, Waterloo would not have been the crushing defeat it was for Napoleon. It would very probably have been a tactical success for Napoleon.

But, on the other hand, we have no ground for thinking that it would have been a final and determining success for the Emperor. For if Wellington had not known quite early in the action that he could count upon the arrival of the Prussians, he would not have accepted battle. If, as a fact, he had found the Prussians intercepted, he could have broken contact and retreated before it was too late.

Had he done so, it would simply have meant that he would later have effected a junction with his allies, and that in the long-run Napoleon would still have had to fight an allied army immensely superior to his own.

All this is as much as to say once more what has been insisted upon throughout these pages; Waterloo was lost, not upon Sunday, June 18th, but two days before, when the 63,000 of Napoleon broke and drove back the 80,000 of Blucher but failed to contain them, failed to drive them eastward, away from Wellington, or to cause a general surrender, and failed because the First French Army Corps, under Erlon, a matter of 20,000 men, failed to come up in flank at the critical moment.

We have seen what the effect of that failure was; we have discussed its causes, and we must repeat the main fact for military history of all those four days: the breakdown of Napoleon's last desperate venture turned upon Erlon's useless marching and countermarching between Quatre Bras and Ligny, two days before the final action of Waterloo was fought.

This being so, the battle of Waterloo must resolve itself into two main phases: the first, the beginning of the struggle with Wellington before the Prussians come up; the second, the main and decisive part of the action, in which both Prussians and English are combined against the French army.

This second phase develops continually as the numbers of the arriving Prussians increase, until it is clinched by the appearance of Ziethen's corps at the very end of the day, and the break-up of the French army; this second part is therefore itself capable of considerable subdivision. But in any large and general view of the whole action, we must regard it as divided into these two great chapters, during the first of which is engaged the doubtful struggle between Napoleon and Wellington; during the second of which the struggle, no longer doubtful, is determined by the arrival of the Prussians in flank upon the field.

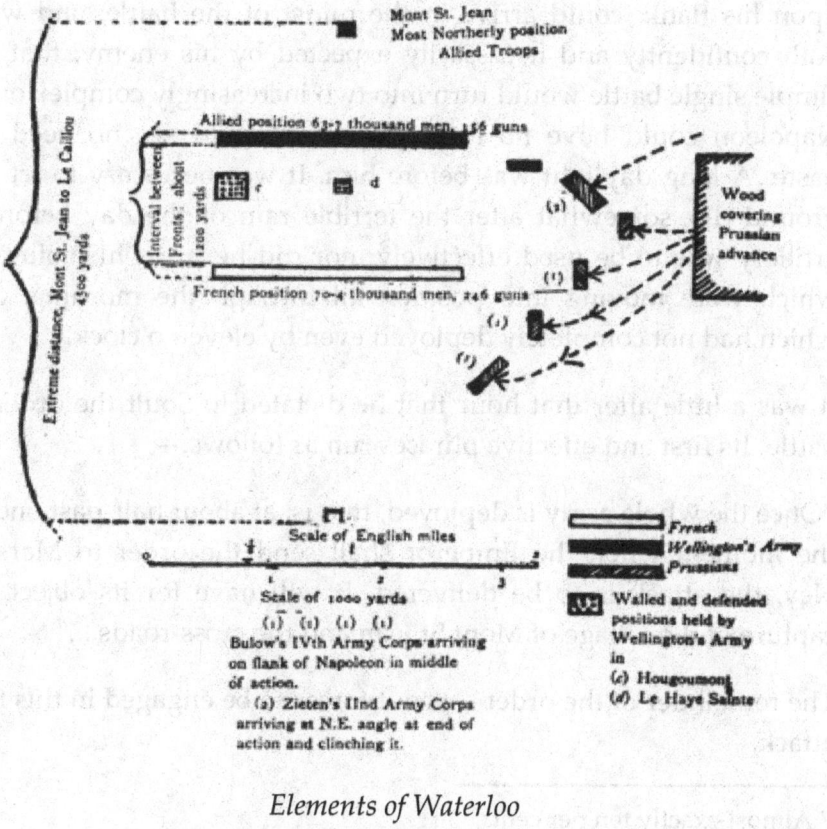

Elements of Waterloo

THE FIRST PART OF THE ACTION

Before the Arrival of the Prussians

The action was to take the form of an assault by Napoleon's forces against this defensive position held by Wellington. It was the business of Wellington, although his total force was slightly inferior to the enemy in numbers,[17] and considerably inferior in guns, to hold that defensive position until the Prussians should come up in flank. This he had had word would take place at latest by one or two o'clock. It was the business of Napoleon to capture the strong outworks, Hougomont and La Haye Sainte; and, that done, to hammer the enemy's line until he broke it. That delay in beginning this hammering would be fatal; that the Prussians were present upon his flank, could arrive in the midst of the battle, and were both confidently and necessarily expected by his enemy; that his simple single battle would turn into two increasingly complex ones, Napoleon could have no idea. Napoleon could see no need for haste. A long daylight was before him. It was necessary to let the ground dry somewhat after the terrible rain of the day before if artillery was to be used effectively; nor did he press his columns, which were moving into position all through the morning, and which had not completely deployed even by eleven o'clock.

It was a little after that hour that he dictated to Soult the order of battle. Its first and effective phrases run as follows:—

"Once the whole army is deployed, that is, at about half-past one, at the moment when the Emperor shall send the order to Marshal Ney, the attack is to be delivered. It will have for its object the capture of the village of Mont St Jean and the cross-roads...."

The remainder of the order sets out forces to be engaged in this first attack.

---

[17] Almost exactly ten per cent.

The French forces consisted in the IInd Army Corps deployed to the left or west of the road, the Ist to the right or east of it, and behind Napoleon, in the centre and in reserve, the VIth Corps and the Guard.

The plan in the Emperor's mind was perfectly simple. There was to be no turning of the right nor of the left flank of the enemy, which would only have the effect of throwing back that enemy east or west. His line was to be pierced, the village of Mont St Jean which lay on the ridge of Wellington's position and which overlooks the plateau on every side was to be carried, and this done Napoleon would be free to decide upon his next action, according to the nature and extent of the disorder into which he had thrown the enemy's broken line.

As a fact, Napoleon made a movement before that hour of half-past one which he had set down in his order for the beginning of the assault. That movement was a movement against the advanced and fortified position of Hougomont.

He sent orders to his left, to the body on the east of the high road, the Second Army Corps, under Reille, to send troops to occupy the outer gardens, wood, and orchards of the country-house, and at twenty-five minutes to twelve the first gun fired in support of that movement was also the first cannonshot of Waterloo.

After a brief artillery duel and exchange of cannonshots between the height on the French left, which overlooks Hougomont, and the corresponding height upon the English right, the French infantry began to march down the slope to occupy the little wood which stands to the south of the chateau. These four regiments were commanded by the Emperor's brother Jerome, who was—as we have seen at Quatre Bras—under the orders of Reille. The clearing of the wood was no very desperate affair, but it was a difficult one, and it took an hour. The Germans of Nassau and Hanover, who were charged with the defence of Hougomont and its approaches, stubbornly contested the standing trees and the cut-clearing which lay between them and the garden wall of the chateau.

It must be clearly seized, at this early and even premature point in the action, that Napoleon's object in making this attack upon Hougomont was only to weaken Wellington's centre.

Hougomont lay upon Wellington's right. Wellington had always been nervous of his right, and feared the turning of his line there, because, should he have to retreat, his communications would ultimately lie in that direction. It was for this reason that he had set right off at Braine l'Alleud, nearly a mile to the west of his line, the Dutch-Belgian Division of Chassé and sixteen guns, which force he connected with a reserve body at Hal, much further to the west.

Napoleon judged that an attack on Hougomont before the action proper was begun, coming thus upon Wellington's right, would make him attempt to reinforce the place and degarnish his centre, where the Emperor intended the brunt of the attack to fall.

Napoleon had no other intention that history can discover in pressing the attack against Hougomont so early. It was almost in the nature of a "feint." But when, towards half-past twelve, his brother's division had cleared the wood and come up against the high garden wall of the farm, for some reason which cannot be determined, whether the eagerness of the troops, the impulsiveness of Jerome himself, or whatever cause, instead of being contented with holding the wood according to orders, the French furiously attacked the loopholed and defended wall. They attempted to break in the great door, which was recessed, and therefore protected by a murderous cross-fire. They were beaten back into the wood, leaving a heap of dead. At this point Reille, according to his own account (which may well enough be accurate), sent orders for the division to remain in the wood, and not to waste itself against so strong an outpost. But Jerome and his men were not to be denied. They marched round the chateau, under a heavy artillery fire from the English batteries above, and attempted to carry the north wall. As they were so doing, four companies of the Coldstreams, the sole reinforcement which Wellington could be tempted to part with from his main line, came in reinforcement to the defence, and, after a sharp struggle, the French were thrust back once more.

It was by that time past one o'clock, and this first furious attempt upon Hougomont, unintended by the Emperor, and a sheer waste, had doubly failed. It had failed in itself—the house and garden still remained untaken, the post was still held. It had failed in its object, which had been to draw Wellington, and to get him to send numerous troops from his centre to his right in defence of the threatened place.

Meanwhile the Emperor, for whom this diversion of a few regiments against Hougomont was but a small matter, had prepared and was about to deliver his main attack.

The reader will see upon the contours of the coloured map a definite spur of land marked with a broad green band in front of the French order of battle, and further marked by the green letter "B" in the very centre of the map. It was along this spur and at about one o'clock that the Emperor drew up a great battery of eighty pieces in order to prepare the assault upon the opposing ridge, which was to be delivered the moment their fire had ceased. Napoleon at that moment was watching his army and its approaching engagement from that summit upon the great road marked "A" in green upon my coloured map, whence the whole landscape to the north and west lies open.[18]

There he received the report of Ney that the guns were ready, and only waiting for the order.

A little while before the guns were ready and Ney had reported to that effect, Napoleon had received Grouchy's letter, in which it was announced that the mass of the Prussian army had retreated on Wavre. He had replied to it with instructions to Grouchy so to act that no Prussian corps at Wavre could come and join Wellington.

---

[18] It is from thirty to fifty feet above the spur on which he had just ranged his guns in front of the army, some twenty-five feet higher than the crest occupied a mile off by the allied army, and a few feet higher than the bare land somewhat more than four miles off, upon which Napoleon first discerned the arriving Prussians.

Hardly had the Emperor dictated this reply when, looking northward and then eastward over the great view, he saw, somewhat over four miles away, a shadow, or a movement, or a stain upon the bare uplands towards Wavre; he thought that appearance to be companies of men. A few moments later a sergeant of Silesian Hussars, taken prisoner by certain cavalry detachments far out to the east, was brought in. He had upon him a letter sent from Bulow to Wellington announcing that the Prussians were at hand, and the prisoner further told the Emperor that the troops just perceived were the vanguard of the Prussian reinforcement. Thus informed, the Emperor caused a postscript to be added to his dictated letter, and bade Grouchy march at once towards this Prussian column, fall upon it while it was still upon the march and defenceless and destroy it.

Such an order presupposed Grouchy's ability to act upon it; Napoleon took that ability for granted. But Grouchy, as a fact, could not act upon it in time. Hard riding could not get Napoleon's note to Grouchy's quarters within much less than an hour and a half. When it got there Grouchy himself must be found, and that done his 33,000 must be got together in order to take the new direction. Further, the Emperor could not know in what state Grouchy's forces might be, nor what direction they might already have taken. It should be mentioned, however, to explain Napoleon's evident hope at the moment of things going well, that *the prisoner had told the Emperor it was commonly believed in the Prussian lines that Grouchy was actually marching to join him, Napoleon, at that moment*. Napoleon sent some cavalry off eastward to watch the advent of the Prussians; he ordered his remnant of one army corps, the Sixth, which he had kept in reserve behind his line, to march down the hill to the village of Plancenoit and stand ready to meet the Prussian attack; and having done all this, he made ready for the assault upon the ridge which Wellington's troops held.

That assault was to be preceded, as I have said, by artillery preparation from the great battery of eighty guns which lay along the spur to the north and in front of the French line. For half an hour those guns filled the shallow valley with their smoke; at half-past one they ceased, and Erlon's First Corps d'Armée, fresh to the combat, because it had so unfortunately missed both Ligny and Quatre Bras, began to descend from its position, to cross the bottom, and to climb the opposite slope, while over the heads of the assaulting columns the French and English cannon answered each other from height to height.

The advance across the valley, as will be apparent from the map, had upon its right the village of Papelotte, upon its left the farm of La Haye Sainte, and for its objective that highway which runs along the top of the ridge, and of which the most part was in those days a sunken road, as effective for defence as a regular trench.

Following a practice which he never abandoned, which he had found universally successful, and upon which he ever relied, the Duke of Wellington had kept his British troops, the nucleus of his defensive plan, for the last and worst of the action. He had stationed to take the first brunt those troops upon which he least relied, and these were the first Dutch-Belgian brigade under Bijlandt. This body was stationed in front of the sunken road (at the point marked A in red upon the map). Behind it he had put Pack's brigade and Kemp's, both British; to the left of it, but also behind the road, Best's Hanoverian brigade. Papelotte village he held with Perponcher's Belgians.

It will be seen that the crushing fire of the French eighty guns maintained for half an hour had fallen full upon the Dutch-Belgians, standing exposed upon the forward slope at a range of not more than 800 yards.[19] At the French charge, though that was delivered through high standing crops and over drenched and slippery soil up the slope, Bijlandt's brigade broke. It is doubtful indeed whether any other troops would not have broken under

---

[19] There is conflict of evidence as to how long the brigade was exposed to this terrible ordeal. It was slightly withdrawn at some moment, but what moment is doubtful.

such circumstances. Unfortunately the incident has been made the subject of repeated and most ungenerous accusation. A body purposely set forward before the whole line to stand such fearful pounding and to shelter the rest; one, moreover, which in two days of fighting certainly lost one-fourth of its number in killed and wounded, and probably lost more than one-third, is deserving of a much more chivalrous judgment than that shown by most historians in its regard. Anyhow, Kemp's brigade quickly filled the gap left by the failure of the Netherlanders, and began to press back the French charge.

Meanwhile the French right, which had captured Papelotte, was compelled to retreat upon seeing the centre thus driven back, while the French left had failed to carry the farm of La Haye Sainte. Indeed upon this side, that is, in the neighbourhood of the great road, the check and reverse to the French assault had been more complete than elsewhere. An attempt to drive its first success home with a cavalry charge had been met by a countercharge, deservedly famous, in which, among other regiments, the First and Second Lifeguards, the Blues, the King's Dragoons, had broken the French horse and followed up the French retirement down the slope. The centre of that retirement was similarly charged by the Scots Greys; and in the end of the whole affair the English horsemen rode up to the spur where the great battery stood, sabred the gunners, and then, being thus advanced so uselessly and so dangerously from their line, were in their turn driven back to the English positions with bad loss.

When this opening chapter of the battle closed, the net result was that the initial charge of the First Corps under Erlon had failed. It had left behind it many prisoners; certain guns which had advanced with it had been put out of action; it had lost two colours.

Save for the furious inconsequent and almost purposeless fighting that was still raging far off to the left round Hougomont, the battle ceased. The valley between the opposing forces was strewn with the dead and dying, but no formed groups stood or moved among the fallen men. The swept slopes had all the appearance during that strange halt of a field already lost or won. The hour was between three and half-past in the afternoon, and so ended the first phase of the battle of Waterloo. It had lasted rather over two hours.

THE SECOND PART OF THE ACTION

The second and decisive phase of the battle of Waterloo differed from the first in this: In the first phase Napoleon was attacking Wellington's command alone. It was line against line. By hammering at the line opposed to him on the ridge of the Mont St Jean, Napoleon confidently expected to break it before the day should close. His first hammer blow, which was the charge of the First Army Corps under Erlon, had failed, and failed badly. The cavalry in support of that infantry charge had failed as well as their comrades, and the British in their turn had charged the retiring French, got right into their line, sabred their gunners, only to be broken in their turn by the counter-effort of further French horse.

This first phase had ended in a sort of halt or faint in the battle, as I have described.

The second phase was a very different matter. It developed into what were essentially two battles. It found Napoleon fighting not only against Wellington in front of him, but against Blucher to his right and almost behind him. It was no longer a simple business of hammering with the whole force of the French army at the British and their allies upon the ridge in front, but of desperately attempting to break the Anglo-Dutch line against time, with diminishing and perpetually reduced forces; with forces perpetually reduced by the necessity of sending more and more men off to the right to resist, if it were possible, the increasing pressure of the accumulating Prussian forces upon the right flank of the French.

This second phase of the action at Waterloo began in the neighbourhood of four o'clock.

It is true that the arriving Prussians had not yet debouched from the screen of wood that hid them two and a half miles away to the east, but at that hour (four o'clock) the heads of their columns were all ready to debouch, and the delay between their actual appearance upon the field and the beginning of the second half of the battle was not material to the result.

That second half of the action began with a series of great cavalry charges which the Emperor had not designed, and which, even as he watched them, he believed would be fatal to him. As spectacles, these famous rides presented the most awful and memorable pageant in the history of modern war; as tactics they were erroneous, and grievously erroneous.

Before this second phase of the battle was entered it was easily open to Napoleon, recognising the Prussians advancing and catching no sight of Grouchy, to change his plan, to abandon the offensive, to stand upon the defensive along the height which he commanded, there to await Grouchy, and, if Grouchy still delayed, to maintain the chances of an issue which might at least be negative, if he could prevent its being decisively disastrous.

But even if such a conception had passed through the Emperor's mind, military science was against it. If ever those opposed to him had full time to concentrate their forces he would, even with the reinforcement of Grouchy, be fighting very nearly two to one. His obvious, one might say his necessary, plan was to break Wellington's line, if still it could be broken, before the full pressure of the arriving Prussians should be felt. Short of that, there could be nothing but immediate or ultimate disaster.

We shall see how, much later in the action, yet another opportunity for breaking away, and for standing upon the defensive, or for retreating, was, in the opinion of some critics, offered to the Emperor by fate.

But we shall see how, upon that second and later occasion in the day, his advantage in so doing was even less than it was now between this hour of half-past three and four o'clock, when he determined to renew the combat.

He first sent orders to Ney to make certain of La Haye Sainte, to clear the enemy from that stronghold, which checked a direct assault upon the centre, and then to renew the general attack.

La Haye Sainte was not taken at this first attempt. The French were repelled; the skirmishers, who were helping the direct attack by mounting the slope upon its right, were thrown back as well, and after this unsuccessful beginning of the movement the guns were called upon to prepare a further and more vigorous assault upon a larger scale. Not only the first great battery of eighty guns, but many of the batteries to the west of the Brussels road (which had hitherto been turned upon Hougomont and the English guns behind that position) were now directed upon the centre of the English line, and there broke out a cannonade even more furious than the one which had opened the action at one o'clock. Men trained in a generation's experience of war called it the most furious artillery effort of their time; and never, perhaps, even in the career of the Gunner who was now in the last extremity of his fate, had guns better served him.

Under the battering of that discharge the front of Wellington's command was partially withdrawn behind the cover of the ridge. A stream of wounded, mixed with not a few men broken and flying, began to swell northward up the Brussels road; and Ney, imagining from such a sight that the enemy's line wavered, committed his capital error, and called upon the cavalry to charge.

Wellington's line was not wavering. For the mass of the French cavalry to charge at such a moment was to waste irreparably a form of energy whose high potential upon the battlefield corresponds to a very rapid exhaustion, and which, invaluable against a front shaken and doubtful, is useless against a front still solid.

It was not and could not have been the Emperor who ordered that false step. It is even uncertain whether the whole body of horsemen that moved had been summoned by Ney, or whether the rearmost did not simply follow the advance of their fellows. At any rate, the great group of mounted men[20] which lay in reserve behind the First Army Corps, and to the west of the road, passed in its entirety through the infantry, and began to advance at the trot down the valley for the assault upon the opposite slope.

I repeat, it is not certain whether Ney called upon all this mass of cavalry and deliberately risked the waste of it in one blow. It is more probable that there was some misunderstanding; that Desnoettes' command, which was drawn up behind Milhaud's, followed Milhaud's, under the impression that a general order had been given to both; that Ney, seeing this extra body of horse following, imagined Napoleon to have given it orders. At any rate, Napoleon never gave such orders, and, from the height upon which he stood, could not have seen the first execution of them, for the first advance of that cavalry was hidden from him by a slight lift of land.

There were 5000 mounted men drawn up in the hollow to the west of the Brussels road for the charge. It was not until they began to climb the slope that Napoleon saw what numbers were being risked, and perceived the full gravity of Ney's error.

To charge unshaken infantry in this fashion, and to charge it without immediate infantry support, was a thing which that master of war would never have commanded, and which, when he saw it

---

[20] The group marked "C" upon the coloured map. It was for the most part under the command of Milhaud, but the rear of it was under the command of Desnoettes.

developing under the command of his lieutenant, filled him with a sense of peril. But it was too late to hesitate or to change the disposition of this sudden move. The 5000 climbed at a slow and difficult trot through the standing crops and the thick mud of the rising ground, suffered—with a moment's wavering—the last discharge of the British guns, and then, on reaching the edge of the plateau, spurred to the gallop and charged.

It was futile. They passed the line of guns (the gunners had orders to abandon their pieces and to retire within the infantry squares); they developed, in too short a start, too slight an impetus; they seethed, as the famous metaphor of that field goes, "like angry waves round rocks"; they lashed against every side of the squares into which the allied infantry had formed. The squares stood.

Wellington had had but a poor opinion of his command. It contained, indeed, elements more diverse and raw material in larger proportion than ever he, or perhaps any other general of the great wars, had had to deal with, but it was infantry hitherto unshaken; and the whole conception of that false movement, the whole error of that cavalry action, lay in the idea that the allied line had suffered in a fashion which it had been very far from suffering. Nothing was done against the squares; and the firmest of them, the nucleus of the whole resistance, were the squares of British infantry, three deep, against which the furious close-sabring, spurring, and fencing of sword with bayonet proved utterly vain. Upon this mass of horsemen moving tumultuous and ineffectual round the islands of foot resisting their every effort, Uxbridge, gathering all his cavalry, charged, and 5000 fresh horse fell upon the French lancers and cuirassiers, already shredded and lessened by grape at fifty yards and musket fire at ten. This countercharge of Uxbridge's cleared the plateau. The French horsemen turned bridle, fled to the hollow of the valley again, and the English gunners returned to their pieces. The whole fury of the thing had failed.

But it had failed only for a moment. What remained of the French horse reformed and once again attempted to charge. Once again, for all their gravely diminished numbers, they climbed the slope; once again the squares were formed, and the torment of horsemen round about them struck once more.

Seen from the point where Napoleon stood to the rear of his line, the high place that overlooked the battlefield, it seemed to eyes of less genius than his own that this second attempt had succeeded. Indeed, its fierce audacity seemed to other than the French observers at that distance to promise success. The drivers of the reserve batteries in the rear of Wellington's line were warned for retreat, and Napoleon, reluctant, but pressed by necessity, seeing one chance at last of victory by mere shock, himself sent forward a reserve of horse to support the distant cuirassiers and lancers. He called upon Kellerman, commanding the cavalry of the Guard, to follow up the charge.

He knew how doubtful was the success of this last reinforcement, for he knew how ill-judged had been Ney's first launching of that great mass of horse at an unbroken enemy; but, now that the thing was done, lest, unsupported, it should turn to a panic which might gain the whole army, he risked almost the last mounted troops he had and sent them forward, acting thus like a man throwing good money after bad for fear that all may be lost.

A better reason still decided Napoleon so to risk a very desperate chance, and to hurl Kellerman upon the heels of Milhaud. That reason was the advent, now accomplished, of the Prussians upon his right, and the necessity, imperative and agonised, of breaking Wellington's line before the whole strength of the newcomers should be felt upon the French flank and rear.

Let us turn, then, and see how far and with what rapidity the Prussians at this moment—nearly half-past five o'clock—had accomplished their purpose.

Of the four Prussian corps d'armée bivouacked in a circle round Wavre, and unmolested, as we have seen, by Grouchy, it was the fourth, that of Bulow, which was given the task of marching first upon the Sunday morning to effect the junction with Wellington. It lay, indeed, the furthest to the east of all the Prussian army,[21] but it was fresh to the fight, for it had come up too late to be engaged at Ligny. It was complete; it was well commanded.

The road it had to traverse was not only long, but difficult. The passage of the river Lasne had to be effected across so steep a ravine and by so impassable a set of ways that the modern observer, following that march as the present writer has followed it, after rain and over those same fields and roads, is led to marvel that it was done in the time which Blucher's energy and the traditional discipline of the Prussian soldiers found possible. At any rate, the heads of the columns were on the Waterloo edge of the Wood of Fischermont[22] (or Paris) before four o'clock, and ready to debouch. Wellington had expected them upon the field by two o'clock at latest. They disappointed him by two hours, and nearly three, but the miracle is that they arrived when they did; and it is well here to consider in detail this feat which the Fourth Prussian Army Corps had accomplished, for it is a matter upon which our historians of Waterloo are often silent, and which has been most unfortunately neglected in this country.

The Fourth Prussian Army Corps, under Bulow, lay as far east as Liège when, on the 14th of June, Napoleon was preparing to cross the Sambre. Its various units were all in the close neighbourhood of the town, so none of them were spared much of the considerable march which all were about to undertake to the west; even its most westward detachment was no more than three miles from Liège city.

Bulow should have received the order to march westward at half-past ten on the morning of the 15th. The order, as we have seen in speaking of Ligny, was not delivered till the evening of that day. The Fourth Army Corps was told to concentrate in the

---

[21] See sketch opposite page 76.
[22] This is the wood upon the extreme right hand of the coloured map.

neighbourhood of Hannut and a little east of that distant point. The corps, as a whole, did not arrive until the early afternoon of Friday the 16th.

It is from this point—Hannut—that the great effort begins.

Bulow, it must be remembered, commanded no less than 32,000 men. The fatigues and difficulties attendant upon the progress of such a body, most of it tied to one road, will easily be appreciated.

During the afternoon of the 16th, while Ligny was being fought, he advanced the whole of this body to points immediately north and east of Gembloux. Not a man, therefore, of his great command had marched less than twenty miles, many must have marched over twenty-five, upon that Friday afternoon.

Then followed the night during which the other three defeated corps fell back upon Wavre.

That night was full of their confused but unmolested retreat. With the early morning of the Saturday Bulow's 32,000 fell back along a line parallel to the general retirement, and all that day they were making their way by the cross-country route through Welhain and Corroy to Dion Le Mont.

This task was accomplished through pouring rain, by unpaved lanes and through intolerable mud, over a distance of close on seventeen miles for the hardest pushed of the troops, and not less than thirteen for those whom the accident of position had most spared.

The greater part of the Fourth Corps had spent the first night in the open; all of it had spent the second night upon the drenched ground. Upon the *third* day, the Sunday of Waterloo, this force, though it lies furthest from the field of Waterloo of all the Prussian forces, is picked out to march first to the aid of Wellington, because it as yet has had no fighting and is supposed to be "fresh." On the daybreak, therefore, after bivouacking in that dreadful weather,

Bulow's force is again upon the move. It does not get through Wavre until something like eight o'clock, and the abominable conditions of the march may be guessed from the fact that its centre did not reach St Lambert until one o'clock, nor did the last brigade pass through that spot until three o'clock. Down the steep ravine of the Lasne and up on the westward side of it was so hard a business that, as we have seen, the brigades did not begin to debouch from the woods at the summit until after four o'clock. It was not until after five o'clock that the last brigade, the 14th, had come up in line with the rest upon the field of Waterloo, having moved, under such abominable conditions of slow, drenched marching, another fifteen miles.

In about forty-eight hours, therefore, this magnificent piece of work had been accomplished. It was a total movement of over fifty miles for the average of the corps—certainly more than sixty for those who had marched furthest—broken only by two short nights, and those nights spent in the open, one under drenching rain. The whole thing was accomplished without appreciable loss of men, guns, or baggage, and at the end of it these men put up a fight which was the chief factor in deciding Waterloo.

Such was the supreme effort of the Fourth Prussian Army Corps which decided Waterloo.

There are not many examples of endurance so tenacious and organisation so excellent in the moving so large a body under such conditions in the whole history of war.

When the Fourth Prussian Corps debouched from the Wood of Fischermont and began its two-mile approach towards his flank, Napoleon, who had already had it watched by a body of cavalry, ordered Lobau with the Sixth French Army Corps, or rather with what he had kept with him of the Sixth Army Corps, to go forward and check it.

It could only be a question of delay. Lobau had but 10,000 against the 30,000 which Bulow could ultimately bring against him when all his brigades had come up; but delay was the essential of the moment to Napoleon. To ward off the advancing Prussian pressure just so long as would permit him to carry the Mont St Jean was his most desperate need. Lobau met the enemy, three to two, in the hollow of Plancenoit,[23] was turned by such superior numbers, and driven from the village.

All this while, during the Prussian success which brought that enemy's reinforcement nearer and nearer to the rear of the French army and to the Emperor's own standpoint, the wasted though magnificent action of the French cavalry was continuing against Wellington's right centre, west of the Brussels road. Kellerman had charged for the third time; the plateau was occupied, the British guns abandoned, the squares formed. For the third time that furious seething of horse against foot was seen from the distant height of the Belle Alliance. For the third time the sight carried with it a deceptive appearance of victory. For the third time the cavalry charge broke back again, spent, into the valley below. Ney, wild as he had been wild at Quatre Bras, failing in judgment as he had failed then, shouted for the last reserve of horse, and forgot to call for that 6000 untouched infantry, the bulk of Reille's Second Corps, which watched from the height of the French ridge the futile efforts of their mounted comrades.

Folly as it was to have charged unbroken infantry with horse alone, the charges had been so repeated and so tenacious that, *immediately* supported by infantry, they might have succeeded. If those 6000 men of Reille's, the mass of the Second Army Corps, which stood to arms unused upon the ridge to the west of the Brussels road, had been ordered to follow hard upon the last cavalry charge, Napoleon might yet have snatched victory from such a desperate double strain as no general yet in military history has escaped. He might

---

[23] In the model on p. 89 Plancenoit is not shown. It would be out of the model, nearer the spectator, behind Napoleon's position at A, and between A and N.

conceivably have broken Wellington's line before that gathering flood of Prussians to the right and behind him should have completed his destruction.

But the moment was missed. Reille's infantry was not ordered forward until the defending line had had ample time to prepare its defence; until the English gunners were back again at their pieces, and the English squares once more deployed and holding the whole line of their height.

It is easy to note such errors as we measure hours and distances upon a map. It is a wonderment to some that such capital errors appear at all in the history of armies. Those who have experience of active service will tell us what the intoxication of the cavalry charges meant, of what blood Ney's brain was full, and why that order for the infantry came too late. Of the 6000 infantry which attempted so belated a charge, a quarter was broken before the British line was reached, and that assault, in its turn, failed.

At this point in the battle, somewhat after six o'clock, two successes on the part of the French gave them an opportunity for their last disastrous effort, and introduced the close of the tragedy.

The first was the capture of La Haye Sainte, the second was the recapture of Plancenoit.

La Haye Sainte, standing still untaken before the very front of Wellington's line, must be captured if yet a further effort was to be attempted by Napoleon. Major Baring had held it with his small body of Germans all day long. Twice had he thrust back a general assault, and throughout more than five hours he had resisted partial and equally unsuccessful attacks. Now Ney, ordered to carry it at whatever cost, brought up against it a division, and more than a division. The French climbed upon their heaped dead, broke the doors, shot from the walls, and, at the end of the butchery, Baring with forty-two men—all that was left him out of nine companies—cut his way back through to the main line, and the farm was taken. Hougomont, on the left, round which so meaningless a struggle had raged all day long, was never wholly cleared of its defenders, but the main body of it was in flames, and with the capture of La Haye Sainte the whole front was free for a final attack at the moment which Napoleon should decide.

Meanwhile, at Plancenoit, further French reinforcements had recaptured the village and again lost it. The Sixth Corps had given way before the Prussian advance, as we have seen. The next French reinforcements, though they had at first thrust the Prussians back, in turn gave way as the last units of the enemy arrived, and the Prussian batteries were dropping shot right on to the fields which bordered the Brussels road.

Napoleon took eleven battalions of the Guard (the Imperial Guard was his reserve, and had not yet come into action[24]) and drew them up upon his flank to defend the Brussels road; with two more battalions he reinforced the wavering troops in Plancenoit. They cleared the enemy out of the village with the bayonet, and for the moment checked that pressure upon the flank and rear which could not but ultimately return.

It was somewhat past seven by the time all this was accomplished. Napoleon surveyed a field over which it was still just possible (in his judgment at least) to strike a blow that might save him. He saw, far upon the left, Hougomont in flames; in the centre, La Haye Sainte captured; on the right, the skirmishers advancing upon the slope before the English line; his eastern flank for the moment free of the Prussians, who had retired before the sudden charge of the Guard. He heard far off a cannonade which might be that of Grouchy.

But even as he looked upon his opportunity he saw one further thing that goaded him to an immediate hazard. Upon the north-eastern corner of his strained and bent-back line of battle, against the far, perilous, exposed angle of it, he saw new, quite unexpected

---

[24] The Guard as a whole had lain behind the French line in reserve all day upon the point marked D upon the coloured map.

hordes of men advancing. It was Ziethen debouching with the head of his First Prussian Army Corps at this latest hour—and Napoleon saw those most distant of his troops ready to yield to the new torrent.

The sun, now within an hour of setting, had shone out again. Its light came level down the shallow valley, but all that hollow was so filled with the smoke of recent discharges that the last stroke which Napoleon was now preparing was in part hidden from the Allies upon the hill. That final stake, the only venture left, was to be use of his last reserve and the charge of the Guard.

No combat in history, perhaps, had seen a situation so desperate maintained without the order for retreat. Wellington's front, which the French were attacking, was still held unbroken; upon the French flank and rear, though the Fourth Prussian Army Corps were for the moment held, they must inevitably return; more remained to come: they were in the act of pressing upon the only line open to the French for retreat, and now here came Ziethen with his new masses upon the top of all.

If, at this hour, just after seven, upon that fatal day, retreat had been possible or advisable to Napoleon, every rule of military art demanded it. He was now quite outnumbered; his exhausted troops were strained up to and beyond the breaking point. To carry such strains too far means in all things, not only in war, an irretrievable catastrophe.

But retreat was hardly possible as a military action; it was impossible as a political one.

Napoleon could hardly retreat at that hour, although he was already defeated, because the fury and the exhaustion of the combat, its increasing confusion, and the increasing dispersion of its units, made any rapid concentration and organisation for the purposes of a sudden retirement hazardous in the extreme. The doomed body, held closer and closer upon its right flank, menaced more and more on its right rear, now suddenly threatened on its exposed salient angle, would fight on.

Though Napoleon had withdrawn from the combat an hour before, when Bülow's 30,000 had struck at his right flank and made his destruction certain; though he had then, while yet he could, organised a retirement, abandoned the furious struggle for La Haye Sainte before it was successful, and covered with his best troops an immediate retreat, that retreat would not have availed his cause.

The appearance of the Prussians on his right proved glaringly the nature of his doom. Grouchy—a quarter of his forces—was cut off from him altogether. The enemy, whom he believed to be beyond Grouchy, and pursued by Grouchy, had appeared, upon the contrary, between Grouchy and himself. Now Ziethen too was here.

Did Napoleon retire, he would retire before forces half as large again as his own, and destined to grow to double his own within a few hours. His retirement would leave Grouchy to certain disaster.

Politically, retreat was still more hopeless. He himself would re-enter France defeated, with, at the most, half the strength that had crossed the frontier three days before. He would so re-enter France—the wealthier classes of which watched his power, nearly all of them with jealousy, most with active hate—surrounded by general officers not ten of whom, perhaps, he could sincerely trust, and by a whole society which supported him only upon the doubtful condition of victory.

Such a retirement was ruin. It was more impossible morally even than it was impossible physically, under the conditions of the field. Therefore it was that, under conditions so desperate, with his battle lost if ever battle was, the Emperor yet attempted one ultimate throw, and in this half-hour before the sunset sent forward the Guard.

In those solemn moments, wherein the Imperial Guard formed for their descent into that hollow whose further slope was to see their last feat of arms, Ziethen, with the First Prussian Corps, pressed on into the far corner the field of battle. At the far end of the long ridge of the Mont St Jean, more than a mile away, this last great body and newest reinforcement of the Emperor's foes had emerged from the walls and thickets of Smohain and, new to the fighting, was already pushing in the weary French line that had stood the carnage of six hours. It was not enough that the Fourth Prussian Corps should have determined the day already with its 30,000 come up from the east against him; now the foremost battalions of the First coming up from the north were appearing to clinch the matter altogether.

It was under such conditions of irretrievable disaster that Napoleon played for miracle, and himself riding slowly down the valley at the head of his comrades and veterans, gave them over to Ney for the final attack against Wellington's line which still held the opposing slope.

It was then, at the moment when Ziethen and the men of the First Prussian Army Corps began to press upon the north-eastern angle of the fight, and were ready to determine it altogether, that the Guard began its ponderous thrust up between Hougomont and La Haye Sainte, to the west of the Brussels road. Up that fatal hill, which had seen the four great cavalry charges, and more recently the breaking of the Second Corps, the tall men, taller for the bearskins and the shouldered musket, the inheritors of twenty-two victorious and now immortal years, leant forward, advancing. To the hanging smoke of the cannon in the vale was added the rising mist of evening; and when the furious cannonade which was to support their attack had ceased with their approach to the enemy's line, a sort of silence fell upon the spectators of that great event.

The event was brief.

It was preceded by a strange sight: a single horseman galloped unharmed from the French to the English line (a captain); he announced to the enemy the approaching movement of the Guard. He was a hater of the flag and of the Revolution, and of its soldier: he was for the old Kings.

There was no need for this dramatic aid. The lull in the action, Napoleon's necessity for a last stroke, possibly through the mist and smoke the actual movement of the Guard, were apparent. The infantry whom Wellington had retired behind the ridge during the worst of the artillery preparation was now set forward again. It was the strongest and the most trusted of his troops whom Wellington posted to receive the shock—Adams' brigade and the brigade of Guards. Three batteries of the reserve were brought forward, with orders not to reply to the French cannon, but to fire at the advancing columns of the charge.

As the Guard went upward, the whole French front to the right moved forward and supported the attack. But upon the left, the Second Army Corps, Reille's recently broken 6000, could not yet move. They came far behind and to the west of the Brussels road; the Guard went up the slope alone.

At two hundred yards from the English line the grape began to mow through them. They closed up after each discharge. Their advance continued unchecked.

Of the four columns,[25] that nearest to the Brussels road reached, touched, and broke the line of the defenders. Its strength was one battalion, yet it took the two English batteries, and, in charging Halkett's brigade, threw the 30th and the 73rd into confusion. It might have been imagined for one moment that the line had here been pierced, but this first and greatest chance of success was defeated, and with it all chances, for it is the head of a charge that tells.

The reader will have seen upon the map, far off to the west or left, at Braine l'Alleud, a body of reserve, Belgian, which Wellington had put so far off in the mistaken notion that the French would try to turn him in that direction. This force of 3000 men with sixteen guns Wellington had recalled in the last phases of the battle. It was their action, and especially that of their artillery, that broke this first

---

[25] Virtually, this advance in echelon had turned into four columns.

success of the Guard. The Netherlanders charged with the bayonet to drive home the effect of their cannon, and the westernmost column of the French attack was ruined.

As the four columns were not all abreast, but the head of the first a little more forward than that of the second, the head of the second than that of the third, and so forth, the shock of the French guard upon the British came in four separate blows, each delivered a few moments later than the last.

We have seen how the Dutch broke the first column.

The second column, which attacked the right of Halkett's brigade, failed also. The 33rd and 69th wavered indeed, but recovered, and their recovery was largely due to the personal courage of their chief.

The next column, again, the third, came upon the British Guards; and the Guards, reserving their fire until the enemy were at a stone's-throw, fired point-blank and threw the French into confusion. During that confusion the brigade of Guards charged, pursued the enemy part of the way down the slope, were closed upon by the enemy and driven back again to the ridge.

The fourth column of the French was now all but striking the extremity of the British line. Here Adams' brigade, a battalion of the 95th, the 71st, and the 52nd regiments, awaited the blow.

The 52nd was the inmost of the three.

It stood just where the confusion of the Guards as they were thrown back up the hill joined the still unbroken ranks of Adams' extremity of the British line.

The 52nd determined the crisis of that day. And it was then precisely that the battle of Waterloo was decided, or, to be more accurate, this was the moment when the inevitable breaking-point appeared.

Colborne was its commander. Instead of waiting in the line, he determined to run the very grave risk of leaving it upon his own initiative, and of playing a tremendous hazard; he took it upon himself to bring the 52nd out, forward in advance of and perpendicular to the defending line, and so to bring a flank fire upon the last French charge.

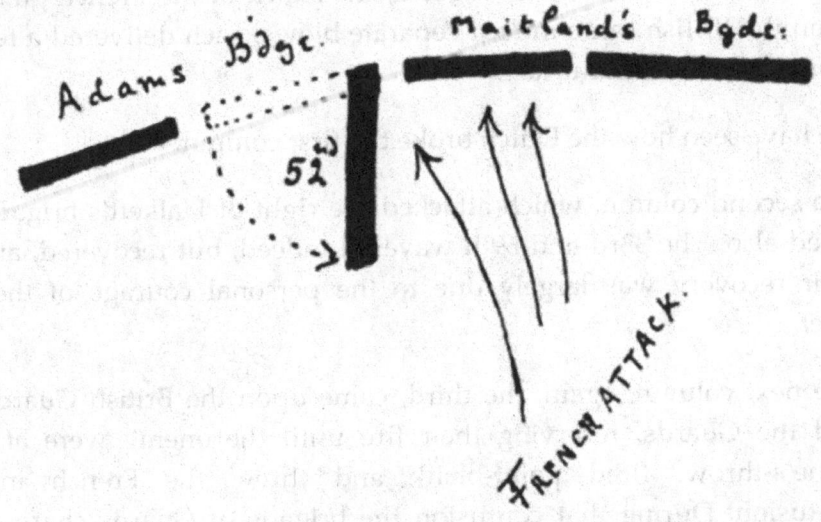

The peril was very great indeed. It left a gap in the English line; the possibility, even the chance, of a French advance to the left against that gap and behind the 52nd meant ruin. It was the sort of thing which, when men do it and fail, is quite the end of them. Colborne did it and succeeded. No French effort was made to the left of the 52nd. It had therefore but its front to consider; it wheeled round, left that dangerous gap in the English line, and poured its fire in flank upon the last charge of the fourth French column. That fire was successful. The assault halted, wavered, and began to break.

The French line to the right, advancing in support of the efforts of the Guard, saw that backward movement, and even as they saw it there came the news of Ziethen's unchecked and overwhelming pressure upon the north-east of the field, a pressure which there also had at last broken the French formation.

The two things were so nearly simultaneous that no historical search or argument will now determine the right of either to priority. As the French west of the Brussels road gave way, the whole English line moved together and began to advance. As the remnants of the First French Army Corps to the east of the Brussels road were struck by Ziethen *they* also broke. At which point the first flexion occurred will never be determined.

The host of Napoleon, stretched to the last limit, and beyond, snapped with the more violence, and in those last moments of daylight a complete confusion seized upon all but two of its numerous and scattered units.

Those two were, first, certain remnants of the Guard itself, and secondly, Lobau's troops, still stubbornly holding the eastern flank.

Squares of the Old Guard, standing firm but isolated in the flood of the panic, checked the pursuit only as islands check a torrent. The pursuit still held. All the world knows the story of the challenge shouted to these veterans, and of Cambronne's disputed reply just before the musket ball broke his face and he fell for dead. Lobau also, as I have said, held his troops together. But the flood of the Prussian advance, perpetually increasing, carried Plancenoit; the rear ranks of the Sixth Army Corps, thrust into the great river of fugitives that was now pouring southward in panic down the Brussels road, were swept away by it and were lost; and at last, as darkness fell, the first ranks also were mixed into the mass of panic, and the Imperial army had ceased to exist.

There was a moon that night; and hour after hour the Prussian cavalry, to whom the task had been entrusted, followed, sabring, pressing, urging the rout. Mile after mile, past the field of Quatre Bras itself, where the corpses, stripped by the peasantry, still lay stark after those two days, the rush of the breakdown ran. Exhaustion had weakened the pursuers before fear had given way to fatigue with the pursued; and when the remnants of Napoleon's army were past the Sambre again, not 30,000 disjointed, unorganised, dispersed, and broken men had survived the disaster.[26]

FINIS

---

[26] We may allow certainly 7000 prisoners and 30,000 killed and wounded, but that is a minimum. It is quite possible that another 3000 should be added to the prisoners and other 5000 to those who fell. The estimates differ so widely because the numerous desertions after the fall of the Empire make it very difficult to compare the remnant of the army with its original strength.

www.ingramcontent.com/pod-product-compliance
Lightning Source LLC
Chambersburg PA
CBHW011255040426
42453CB00015B/2422